TAOISM, TEACHING, AND LEARNING

A Nature-Based Approach to Education

The ancient Chinese philosophy of Taoism contains profound wisdom about the cosmos, nature, human life, and education. Taoism seeks to be in harmony with nature, and using it as a guide can help us live in a way that is healing to both ourselves and the planet.

Taoism, Teaching, and Learning identifies key aspects of Taoist thought and highlights how these principles can promote a holistic approach to teaching and learning. In particular, this book offers educators guidelines and pedagogical examples for how to instil a perspective of interconnectedness into their classrooms. It sheds light on how philosophical Taoism articulates a vision of the universe and life that mirrors the actual realities of nature.

Providing frameworks and methods for teaching and learning based on the interconnectedness of life, *Taoism, Teaching, and Learning* develops an inspiring vision for education and helps us to see our world in a deeply holistic and meaningful way.

JOHN P. MILLER is a professor in the Department of Curriculum, Teaching, and Learning at the University of Toronto.

XIANG LI earned her MEd in curriculum and pedagogy from the Ontario Institute for Studies in Education at the University of Toronto.

TIAN RUAN earned her MEd in curriculum and pedagogy from the Ontario Institute for Studies in Education at the University of Toronto.

TAOISM, TEACHING, AND LEARNING

A Nature-Based Approach to Education

John P. Miller
With Xiang Li and Tian Ruan

UNIVERSITY OF TORONTO PRESS
Toronto Buffalo London

© University of Toronto Press 2022
Toronto Buffalo London
utorontopress.com

ISBN 978-1-4875-4094-4 (cloth)   ISBN 978-1-4875-4097-5 (EPUB)
ISBN 978-1-4875-4095-1 (paper)   ISBN 978-1-4875-4096-8 (PDF)

Library and Archives Canada Cataloguing in Publication

Title: Taoism, teaching, and learning : a nature-based approach to education / John P.
   Miller with Xiang Li and Tian Ruan.
Names: Miller, John P., 1943–, author. | Li, Xiang (Researcher in education), author. |
   Ruan, Tian, author.
Identifiers: Canadiana (print) 20220172439 | Canadiana (ebook) 20220172579 |
   ISBN 9781487540944 (hardcover) | ISBN 9781487540951 (softcover) |
   ISBN 9781487540968 (PDF) | ISBN 9781487540975 (EPUB)
Subjects: LCSH: Holistic education. | LCSH: Taoist philosophy. | LCSH: Taoism. |
   LCSH: Education.
Classification: LCC LC990 .M55 2022 | DDC 370.11 – dc23

Every effort has been made to contact copyright holders; in the event of an error or
omission, please notify the publisher.

We wish to acknowledge the land on which the University of Toronto Press
operates. This land is the traditional territory of the Wendat, the Anishnaabeg, the
Haudenosaunee, the Métis, and the Mississaugas of the Credit First Nation.

University of Toronto Press acknowledges the financial support of the Government
of Canada, the Canada Council for the Arts, and the Ontario Arts Council, an agency
of the Government of Ontario, for its publishing activities.

**Canada Council Conseil des Arts
for the Arts du Canada**

ONTARIO ARTS COUNCIL
CONSEIL DES ARTS DE L'ONTARIO
an Ontario government agency
un organisme du gouvernement de l'Ontario

Funded by the Financé par le
Government gouvernement
of Canada du Canada

Canadä

Contents

Foreword

Taoism contains profound wisdom about the cosmos, nature, human life, and education. There are many books on Tao and its applications in every facet of our lives. Taoist learning is often combined with our inner work involving cultivation of energy and spirit and a world view of interconnection positing a universe that is creative and intelligent. Dr. John Miller (who goes by the name Jack) is a wonderful scholar whose writing has positive energy and embraces the spirit of the Tao. It is always a joy reading his and his collaborators' work. This one is no exception. Many parts of the book are just beautiful to read, illuminating wisdom and elegance.

Jack Miller, Xiang Li, and Tian Ruan attempt to "reset" education, positing that we live in an interconnected world, one in which the cosmos, earth, and human beings are inextricably linked by Tao, the creative force and energy of all existence. The book touches on the main essence of Taoist teaching, for example, qi, harmony, balance, virtues, self-cultivation, *wu-wei* (following the way of Tao effortlessly and with grace), and respect for nature. What makes the book stand out is that these Taoist concepts are made concrete and come to life through vivid examples, enabling readers to experience and envision what the Tao of teaching and learning is like.

The authors help us envision a new form of education based on Taoist philosophy. Discussed are journeys inward to connect with our inner spirit and with nature. Through inner work and cultivation, we are much better equipped to educate for well-being, wholeness, compassion and wisdom. Chapter 1 by Xiang Li focuses on teaching Taoist philosophy through a classical Suzhou garden. The chapter is a nice introduction to Taoism, providing down-to-earth knowledge such as the notion of *yin* and *yang*, and Taoist spiritual practices. The example of the student club learning in a Taoist heritage garden is very interesting, illustrating how children can connect with nature if service learning, experiential learning, and inquiry-based education are integrally provided. In chapters 2–6, Jack cites from various philosophers and Taoist texts. His insights are refreshing. Jack offers his own experience of guiding teachers to do meditation and develop insights. He shares what the teachers experienced and the impact of doing meditation practice. He critiques the imbalances in our education, such as focusing on content not process, knowledge not imagination, and the rational not the intuitive. He offers great ideas about how we can balance the yin and yang of school curriculum. Chapter 7 by Tian Ruan provides vivid descriptions of how she employed "play pedagogies" that are child-centred. Her teaching promotes students' holistic development and creativity through joyful and effortless play. The last chapter concludes the book with concerns for climate change and posits love as the underlying energy that sustains all life forms. It is very profound and elevating.

The book provides wonderful insights on Taoism and its wisdom for education. It is very timely for our world. Teachers can gain a lot from this book, such as practices for aligning their body, mind, heart, spirit, and qi, achieving calmness, tranquility, mindfulness, and deep knowing. Jack and his co-authors illustrate how to balance yin and yang in education, how wu-wei manifests in teachers' pedagogies, such as teaching with spontaneity and grace and leaving space open for creative imagination and play. During the COVID-19 shut-down period when I was writing this, I was imagining what a world we could have if Tao was fully integrated into our life and education. It is high time we educate future generations to harbour and live the wisdom of Tao.

Jing Lin

Preface

I first became interested in Taoism as a young American in the 1960s when I was facing the draft and the Vietnam War; I was searching for ways to deal with the stress of that time. I started the practice of yoga and I became interested in Eastern thought and Taoism. Stephen Mitchell's 1988 translation of the *Tao Te Ching* reignited my interest in Taoism when it was published. The work of Thomas Cleary then opened me to more Taoist writings.

During the summer of 2019 I taught my course, the Holistic Curriculum, and there were several Chinese students in the class. They did a presentation on Chinese philosophy that inspired me to explore writing a book on Taoism with the help of two students in that class, Tian Ruan and Xiang Li. As we were working on the last part of this book, the COVID-19 pandemic occurred. Like most places, Toronto was shut down so the virus would not spread. Some people have suggested that this period has been an opportunity to look closely at our society and ourselves and to chart a new course. Education needs to start from a place where the cosmos, the earth, and our lives are seen as interconnected and sacred. One Chinese scholar has written: "We understand that what is regarded as sacred is more likely to be treated with care and respect. Our planetary home should be so regarded. Efforts to safeguard and cherish the environment need to be infused with a vision of the sacred" (quoted in Tu, Weming, and Tucker 2004, 497).

Taoism can help us see our world in this way and can also help us develop a new vision for education. Together with Indigenous wisdom and the type of love and non-violence that Martin Luther King Jr. and

Mahatma Gandhi articulated, there can be a multifaceted, inclusive vision that can guide us towards an education that can help heal ourselves and the planet. This vision can be a starting point in trying to find a way of teaching and learning that inspires young people in what Thomas Berry wrote about in his book, *The Great Work: Our Way into the Future* (1999).

This book begins with Xiang's chapter, "Exploring Taoist Educational Philosophies in a Classical Suzhou Garden." This is followed by my chapters on Taoism, self-cultivation, wu-wei, yin and yang, and holistic education. Tian's chapter focuses on yin and yang and the role of play in kindergarten. The book closes with a new vision for education.

I am so grateful that University of Toronto Press is publishing another book of mine. Special thanks to Meg Patterson for guiding the review process of the manuscript. I am also grateful to Janice Evans for managing its editing and production. Also thanks to Beth McAuley of The Editing Company for her careful copyediting of the book. I am grateful to Rupert Collister, a colleague and friend, who proofed an early version of the manuscript.

TAOISM, TEACHING, AND LEARNING

A Nature-Based Approach to Education

Chapter One

Exploring Taoist Educational Philosophies in a Classical Suzhou Garden

Xiang Li

In this chapter, I first describe my own experience and understanding of Taoism growing up in China and then my experience working with students in an historical Suzhou garden.

In my childhood, I was told many Taoist stories by my grandma. Most of them were ancient Chinese folktales. What fascinated me most were the stories of Taoist priests, who usually lived in a mountain hermitage, far away from the chaos of people. They were often presented as sage elders, dressed in Taoist robes, wearing an unfathomable smile. They practised Taoist self-cultivation and alchemy day by day, to attain supernatural powers, even immortality. The climax of the story always came when the priests went down the mountain to expel the mysterious monsters that threatened the common people. The priest slowly blew some air, then the monster that took a human form immediately revealed its real face, and was finally defeated. I was captivated by these legendary tales.

When Chinese New Year came, my grandma always bought some posters that featured the Door God and the Kitchen God, two important Taoist Gods who are believed to protect the household and bring them auspiciousness. Families are supposed to replace the old posters with the new one on New Year's Eve, to bid farewell to the past year and welcome a prosperous new year. When the birthday of the Kitchen God arrived, my grandma served hearty food as offerings to him, because the Kitchen God goes back to the heaven once a year to report every detail of the family to the Jade Emperor (the highest Taoist God). These Taoist folk customs are still widely practised today in most rural areas of China.

As I grew older, I read more Taoist allegories adapted from Taoist classics, such as *Tao Te Ching* and *Chuang Tsu* (see S. Mitchell 1988, and Chuang

Tsu 1974, respectively; see also Merton 1965; Watson 1968). The most impressive one was Chuang-Tzu's butterfly dream: Chuang-Tzu dreamt he was a butterfly. After awakening, he couldn't distinguish between reality and illusion. He was unsure whether it was him who dreamed he was a butterfly, or it was a butterfly who dreamed he was Chuang-Tzu. Back at that time, I couldn't fully comprehend the profound philosophical implications, but I remember how amazed I was by the romanticism of the story. From then on, I regarded Taoism as romantic, poetic, and somewhat mystic.

About three years ago, I finally got a chance to visit a mountain sacred to Taoists, Mount Lao, in Qingdao. Mount Lao is renowned as one of the birthplaces of Taoism in China, with a history dating back to the Spring and Autumn Period (771 to 476 BC) over two thousand years ago. With a vast land jutting out into the sea, the mountain is blessed with spectacular mountainous and ocean sceneries. The isolated seaside location also makes it an ideal place for Taoist priests and nuns to live in seclusion. I went to Mount Lao on an early spring day. The bus made its way slowly along the coastal road, with the verdant, mist-covered mountains on one side, and the emerald-green sea on the other. The mountains, fog, light, and sea were linked together in the distance, melting into the sky. The scene in front of me was just like the hermitage I had pictured in my childhood. The road ended at the foot of the mountain, where stood a Taoist temple with a millennium-long history, the Taiqing Palace. It is the largest and most famous Taoist complex among the surviving Taoist temples on Mount Lao.

The crisp mountain air and salty sea breeze quickly refreshed me. Looking around, I found that the temple was built facing the sea and against the mountains, which was regarded as a superb location according to Chinese *feng shui* (the principles of living in harmony with the surrounding environment). A massive statue of Lao Tzu perched on the mountainside, with one index finger pointing up to the sky, and with the other one pointing down to the earth. This gesture might symbolize the Taoist cosmology that Tao is the origin of heaven, earth, and all beings. This concept is explained by Lao-Tzu in *Tao Te Ching*, chapter 42: "The Tao gives birth to One (universe). One gives birth to Two (of Yin and Yang). Two gives birth to Three (of Heaven, Earth, and Human). Three gives birth to all things" (see S. Mitchell 1988). A stone path lined with towering pine trees led me to the main hall of the temple. The atmosphere here was very different from the Buddhist temples that I had been to. In a Buddhist temple, the hall is always flooded with the large crowds, the sounds of monks chanting, and the heavy fragrance of incense. It was much quieter here. The strings of small chimes tinkled gently in the breeze. Only several pilgrims were praying to the deities. A Taoist priest was interpreting a fortune stick to an advice-seeker, smilingly and patiently. The aroma of incense, mingled with the scent of plants, drifted through the room. I naturally closed my eyes to savour this moment of peace and tranquility.

Stepping out of the main hall, I heard some enchanting music. A Taoist priest was sitting on a stone stool under an ancient cypress tree, playing the erhu (a traditional Chinese two-stringed instrument). He wore a dark blue Taoist robe, with his long hair coiled into a bun on top of his head. Behind him stood a big rock carved with the words quoted from *Tao Te Ching*: "The Tao follows only itself" (*dao fa zi ran*, chapter 25). The priest noticed me and nodded at me in a friendly way. He told me that if I had come earlier in the morning, I could have enjoyed an authentic Taoist music performance. The priest added that nowadays, they do more than just practise religious rituals, like staging ceremonies on Taoist festivals. They also offer Taoist cultural exploration opportunities, such as traditional kung fu, tai chi, qigong, and meditation training. He suggested I visit the back mountain where the training took place.

The back mountain was even more secluded with very few visitors. Against the silence, I could hear birds tweeting, leaves rustling, and streams burbling. Small waterfalls cascaded down the rock outcrops, plunging into the colourful ponds, where the exuberant spring flowers and trees were reflected. It had been a long time since I could relish a moment of solitude and appreciate the beauty of nature wholeheartedly. Walking along the winding mountain path, I came across a group of people practising tai chi, a Taoist martial art that aids the flow of instinct energy or *qi*.

Following a Taoist priest's demonstration, the practitioners imitated the movements slowly, inhaling and exhaling breaths relaxingly. Their Taoist robes fluttered when they turned and stretched, like white butterflies. A humble bungalow was located just steps away, next to a patch of green farmland. The house was the priests' residence, which demonstrated their minimalist and self-sufficient lifestyle. I was not surprised to spot several young people within the tai chi group. Nowadays, younger generations show increasing interest in attending this type of Taoist wellness retreat in a temple. Here they do several hours of meditation a day, eat light natural food, and engage in Taoist physical exercises. Taoism offers these young people a refuge from the hectic urban life, where they can immerse themselves in nature, clear the mind, and restore the balance of inner-energy through Taoist practices.

After the trip to Mount Lao, I felt Taoism was no longer that mystical and unreachable. It is a way of living, a philosophy of life. In the modern era when fortune, fame, and power are highly valued, Taoism seems to be "rebellious." Taoist culture persuades people to stop forcing things, to let things be, and to follow their instincts. Taoism calls for reconnecting with nature and living in harmony with nature, and by doing so, to retrieve the inner peace and tranquility. Modern Taoists are propagating Taoist philosophy through hosting tai chi, qigong, meditation, and other Taoist practices, which offer people a means to relieve stress and appreciate the wisdom of Taoism.

The Influence of Taoist Philosophy on Chinese People

Taoism, as an indigenous Chinese religion and philosophy, has profoundly shaped Chinese people's world view and lifestyle. Although China has experienced rapid urban growth during the past several decades, many people still long to escape from the concrete jungle and return to nature. In the depths of their hearts, there exists a peaceful land called "Southern Mount" (*Nan Shan*). Southern Mount is a place depicted in the poem "Drinking Wine No. 5" by one of China's most celebrated poets Tao Yuanming (AD 365–427). Tao was a government official during the East Jin Dynasty (AD 317–420). Due to his disgust with political strife and corrupt government, he chose to resign from the civil service and live in solitude on his farm (Palandri 1988). After finishing building his new home, he wrote:

> I build my house amid the bustling world,
> Yet I cannot hear the noise of carriages and horses.
> People ask me how I achieve this,
> My heart is secluded, so is my place.

While plucking chrysanthemums by the eastern fences,
I carefreely gaze at the Southern Hill.
The mountain air against the sunset is so pleasant,
The birds fly back home in flocks.
This scene must reveal some truth,
But words fail to explain. (translation by Xiang Li)

In this poem, Tao expresses his heartfelt joy after returning to nature and living an idyllic life. He leisurely gazes at the Southern Mount and plucks wildflowers near the eastern hedge, feeling completely free and peaceful. The poet shows much Taoist influence in this poem. His desire for following his instinct and living in harmony with nature accords with Taoism's principle *ziran* (naturalness; spontaneity). His lack of political ambition and carefree lifestyle also correspond to the Taoist philosophy *wu-wei* (effortless action; not forcing; going with the flow). Following Tao Yuanming, many Chinese poets and painters draw their inspiration from Taoist philosophy. "With-draw-from-society," "return to nature," and "reclusive life" have become conventional themes of Chinese poetry, painting, and calligraphy.

Taoism believes that the human being is an integral part of nature. This idea was expressed in chapter 25 of the *Tao Te Ching*: "The Tao is great. The universe is great. Earth is great. Man is great. These are the four great powers. Man follows the earth. Earth follows the universe. The universe follows the Tao. The Tao follows only itself." Taoism suggests that men and women follow the laws of nature with deep reverence. Guided by this insight, Chinese people place a high value on the idea of harmony between humanity and nature. One good example is *jieqi*. Over two thousand years ago, the ancient Chinese created the Twenty-Four Solar Terms (jieqi), which divides a year into twenty-four segments based on the observations of the sun's annual motion. Jieqi guides farmers during agricultural production, and reminds city people of nature's cycles and teaches them how to live in harmony with nature. It is believed that changes in nature have a substantial effect on our body and mood, so Chinese people developed a set of solar term traditions featuring healthy living habits that correspond to the flow of nature. For example, one should follow a proper diet during a specific segment of the year and adjust his/her daily routine in accordance with the changing seasons. Feng shui is another excellent example of living in alignment with nature. Feng shui literally means wind and water, two primary components of nature. The practice of feng shui refers to the arrangement of furniture, buildings, and space in harmony with the surrounding natural environment. Good feng shui is thought to promote positive energy and bring about good fortune. In ancient China, major cities and important buildings were all built following the principles of feng shui. Until today, many Chinese, especially those from South China, still consult feng shui masters about real estate purchases, home decorations, even tomb locations.

Another essential component of Taoism is balance. The Taoist yin-yang symbol is a firm reminder of this. In Chinese, yin translates into "femininity, shade" while yang translates into "masculinity, sun." Although yin and yang represent two opposing natural forces, they are not entirely separate; they are fluid and interconnected. The two halves are continually changing and intertwining, reaching a state of balance as a whole. In the *Tao Te Ching*, chapter 42, Lao-Tzu said, "All things have their backs to the female, and stand facing the male. When male and female combine, all things achieve harmony." However, human minds tend to think in an absolute and static way. When we are faced with adversity (yin), we cling to neglect the opportunities (yang) contained in the crisis. When we enjoy the happiness of success (yang), we are unaware of the accumulative stress (yin) it causes. Taoism teaches us to change this mindset and start to look at the world as a whole. If we can appreciate the complex inter-relatedness and interdependence of everything in life, we will attain the inner balance and harmony.

Deeply rooted in the Taoist yin-yang philosophy, Traditional Chinese Medicine (TCM) seeks to maintain the body's yin-yang balance to achieve physical and mental health. Two thousand years ago, Chinese medical books had already categorized nine human body constitutions based on the individual's yin and yang energy (Sun et al. 2018). It is believed that the unbalanced condition of yin and yang will result in uncomfortableness and disease. For instance, people of yin-deficient (*yinxu*) type (whose yang energy is higher than yin energy) are prone to have dryness problems and ulcers. In contrast, people of yang-deficient (*yangxu*) type (whose yin energy is excessive) are susceptible to puffiness and stomach chills. These symptoms alert people to take active measures to restore balance in the body by modifying lifestyles, adjusting mental states, and doing proper exercises.

Taoist exercises such as qigong and tai chi are widely practised in China as a means of nourishing the inner balance. Unlike traditional Western workouts that aim at calorie burning through high-intensity training, qigong and tai chi stress stillness and serenity. During tai chi or qigong practise, people move very slowly, focusing primarily on their breaths and bodily sensations. Taoists hold the view that tai chi and qigong can promote the smooth flow of qi, a type of instinct energy in our body, which is essential to stay healthy and achieve longevity. Compared with sheer physical exertion, Taoist cultivation integrates contemplative practices and physical exercises, which is more effective in managing anxiety and helping the body return to balance. Heavily influenced by Taoist beliefs, the Chinese prefer quiet leisure activities rather than strenuous ones (Wang and Stringer 2011). Whether practising tai chi, performing a tea ceremony, writing calligraphy, or merely taking a walk in the park, the Chinese enjoy all kinds of activities that can bring them peace and tranquility. When doing these activities, people can easily concentrate on their inner spiritual world, letting go of the external matters, which allows them to come into a healthy balance of mind and body.

Taoist Wisdom in Education

Taoism is one of the most prevalent philosophies in Chinese society, with many of its teachings being applied to multiple areas of life. Governors take strategic advice from Taoism to run the country; artists and litterateurs turn to Taoism for fresh inspiration; medical scientists create regimens based on Taoism; ordinary people absorb endless wisdom from Taoism to nourish bodies and souls. In recent years, some scholars have directed their attention to connecting Taoist philosophy with education. Miller (2019a) develops the theory of holistic curriculum inspired by the Taoist philosophy yin-yang balance. He argues that "Western culture and education has been dominated by the *yang* which tends to emphasize the rational, the material, the masculine, and the individual to the exclusion of the intuitive, the spiritual, the feminine, and the group. This imbalance one could argue has led to sickness in the culture and institutions including education" (Miller 2019a, 13). Holistic curriculum attempts to balance the yin and yang, to build the interconnectedness of different aspects in education, and to nurture the whole child. A Chinese scholar, Fan Yang, relates the *Tao Te Ching* to individualized teaching and learning. Taoism advocates diversity and encourages people to adhere to their pure naturalness. Reflecting on its pedagogical implication, Yang (2018) notes that "each student has unique potential talents, individual needs, and a personal learning style," and educators need to "provide different proposals that recognize those differences, to design a suitable teaching plan for each student, and to use multiple criteria to help each student grow" (8).

Taoism provides a vision for what education could be like. A Taoist classroom will be without walls. It can be in the mountain, by the stream. Students will learn about the laws of nature by observing a seed breaking through the soil, or a butterfly emerging from its chrysalis. Students have the autonomy to decide what they want to explore by their interests and learn naturally through their own experience. During this process, they will learn to respect and care for the world and others. Most importantly, they will learn about themselves. They will discover their uniqueness, be more aware of their emotions, and feel comfortable in their own skin. In this way, they can sincerely embrace their naturalness and harmonize with the Tao. The Taoist classroom, however, seems to be too idealistic in contemporary educational settings. I grew up in an educational system that was standardized-test-oriented, teacher-dominated, with an overriding emphasis on academic excellence, and this system did not change substantially until today. As an educator who appreciates Taoist wisdom, I have always been experimenting with incorporating Taoist philosophical ideas into my teaching.

Back in 2014, I had just graduated from college and started my first job in a high school in Suzhou, an historic and beautiful city in East China. I was an English teacher, also a homeroom teacher for a ninth-grade class of thirty students. Like every first-time teacher, I was very excited to stand in front of so many curious eyes and get to know these interesting souls. Meanwhile, I felt nervous about the upcoming and unknown challenges. My students were only six to seven years younger than me, so I had to walk a fine line between being their teacher and being their friend. For a new teacher, it was tough to develop a close rapport with the students while not undermining my authority. In the beginning, I carefully hid my real personality and wore a serious face every day. But shortly after, I found I couldn't help revealing who I was to my students. I couldn't help smiling or laughing, telling anecdotes about the famous writers in the textbook, talking with my students during breaks, and sharing my life experience. Finally, I decided to simply be myself.

Every Thursday afternoon, students had two hours for their student club activities. Each teacher would be assigned to a club as a supervisor. This was one of the most anticipated moments in my first week of teaching. I was looking forward to being assigned to something interesting, such as an anime club or a choir club, but when I got the assignment sheet, I was bewildered. I was assigned to the "World Heritage Club." What does this club do? I immediately sought help from my colleague, the former supervisor of this club. "Nothing special," she replied flatly. "We watched some documentaries about world heritage sites. You know, the students preferred to finish earlier then go back home." "That's it?" I tried to cover my disappointment. "Oh, we visited the Humble Administrator's Garden at the end of the term." My eyes lit up.

Suzhou is famous for its classical gardens, and among which, the Humble Administrator's Garden is the biggest and the most renowned. This five-hundred-year-old garden was originally built by a government official during the Ming Dynasty (1368–1644) and was taken over by twenty owners. Today, it is listed as a UNESCO World Cultural Heritage site and is a major historical and cultural site protected at the national level. However, with accelerated urban development, the light of this cultural treasure was dimming. Skyscrapers had replaced the historic neighbourhood, and young people were gradually losing interest in the traditional culture. I was so upset reading about the decline of this exquisite garden. I hoped youngsters could do something for it. I came up with a plan for the new World Heritage Club.

On Thursday, I walked into the club activity room at a brisk pace. As I expected, only eight students were sitting in the room (the number grew to twelve the next week). When I said that we would mostly be out of the school during the club hours, their weary eyes started to sparkle with enthusiasm and excitement. Earlier that week, I had contacted the administrative office of the Humble Administrator's Garden about doing volunteer and research activities in the garden. Thankfully, the individual

I spoke with was very supportive. We later discussed the itinerary of the first student visit and the follow-up activities. I also got permission from the school to make field trips during the club hours. I told the students that they would mainly spend the club time at the Humble Administrator's Garden and that they would be doing some volunteer work and group research there. The classroom burst into cheers. I added that they needed to record photos and videos to demonstrate what they observed, felt, and learned. At the end of this project, they would give a presentation about their volunteer experience. And, most importantly, they would probe into how to *better* preserve and promote this old garden and present their research results.

Two weeks later, we took our first trip to the Humble Administrator's Garden. The director gave us a guided tour around the garden. Everyone, including myself, was amazed by the superb craftsmanship of our ancestors. Then five volunteers gave us a brief presentation on World Heritage Sites and the Humble Administrator's Garden. They also introduced the volunteer work at the garden. The head of volunteers was an amiable senior man, who had been volunteering there for several decades. It was touching to see people of different ages, from all walks of life, devoted to protecting this historical legacy. For the next two months, we came here almost every Thursday. The students rotated on two different volunteer roles, tour guide and assistant to the conservation specialist. Gradually, they formed small groups to work together. Some groups also spent extra time volunteering on weekends. At the end of the semester, every group shared their volunteer experience and their thoughts about how to preserve this garden better and attract younger tourists. We presented our club activities to the other teachers, students, and parents on the School Club Day. Looking back on this experience, I believe it demonstrated some possibilities of connecting Taoism with contemporary education.

Let Nature Be the Teacher

Taoism holds that humans are only a part of the grand cosmos, like all other beings. We all follow Tao, which requires us to live in harmony with nature. When it comes to teaching about nature, sometimes we teachers are too confident. We present our students with some pictures and video clips on the projector screens, and we expect these inanimate images to connect our students with nature's rhythm. We hope our students can develop an abiding love for life, but in fact, they are losing the ability to resonate with the natural world. How can we align our students with the natural laws again, if we isolate them within the bounded walls of the classroom? We ought to first guide them to experience nature. We should always keep in mind that nature is the greatest teacher of all.

The Chinese-American architect Ieoh Ming Pei, the creator of the Louvre Pyramid, once said that he drew inspiration from his childhood "playground," the Shizilin (Lion Grove) Garden in Suzhou (Leung 2019). Like Pei, the students found inspiration in the five-hundred-year-old Humble Administrator's Garden. A garden can teach enormous things to a child, more than any wise and experienced teacher can. During their visits there, the students listened attentively to the guide explaining the historical facts, architecture style, and cultural connotations, falling all over each other to raise questions. I had rarely seen my students so focused and eager to learn. They touched every calligraphy carved into the stone, read out the antithetical couplets on the doors, and argued about the meaning of the sentences written in ancient Chinese. They pored over each explanation board of the site, imagining the ancients' way of life over the past five centuries. The students were more than absorbing knowledge; they were savouring the garden, feeling the poetic soul of it. The history, literature, art, and culture were no longer imparted by the monotonous facts and numbers in the textbook, but by the flowers, leaves, pavilions, bridges, stones, and bricks. They were all vividly telling the stories.

In the first several weeks, I noticed that some students checked their cellphones from time to time when they were pruning the trees and weeding. After one month, they started to ignore their phones and began to pay the utmost attention to what they were doing. They gently cut off the withered twigs, saddened by the end of life. They applauded when discovering a new-germinated stem, amazed by the pulsing vitality of life. Through taking care of the plants, students started to reconnect to nature and recapture the cosmic energies. I was not surprised when I heard some of my students commenting that they enjoyed this work. They were relaxed when they put aside the distracting thoughts and fully concentrated on the work at hand. The earthy aroma of the soil made them feel calm and peaceful. Their experience showed how nature restores and heals.

There were two old ginkgo trees in the central section of the garden. On a tranquil autumn afternoon, a boy suddenly pointed to them and, calling me by the name I use as an English teacher, told me excitedly, "Olivia, look! They turn yellow!" I lifted my head, letting my eyes soak in the golden waves. A heady fragrance of the osmanthus trees wafted through the air. The boy closed his eyes and took a deep breath. I suddenly noticed that something had changed imperceptibly. Then, a day or later, when we were about to leave, a girl gave me a beautiful bookmark made of pressed plants. She had collected the fallen leaves and flowers in the garden and eternalized their beauty before they decomposed into the soil. I realized that these young people were now more sensitive to the charms of nature. They had more time to detach from their high-tech gadgets and purify their mind by appreciating the ripples in the pond, the sound of the wind, and the shadows of the trees.

The design of the Humble Administrator's Garden embodies the traditional Taoist philosophical ideas of "Nature and Man in One" and "Harmony between Nature and Human" (Cui and Hu 2015). This design concept was introduced to the students during their first visit, but at that time, they couldn't fully comprehend the deep meaning of the phrase. After several weeks of immersing themselves in this old garden, they started developing an emotional bond with each flower, stone, and bridge, as these things constituted their childhood wonderland. They were later genuinely caring for this garden, like caring for an old friend, because they were more aware of the vulnerability of everything here. I started to feel that these young people became more responsible for what they were doing. They discreetly watched visitors passing by and kindly reminded them not to cross the marked lines on the floor or not to lean on the stone pillars. At that moment, they put themselves on an equal position as a flower, a tree, a stone in the garden. And this was the time when they finally understood "Nature and Man in One" and perceived the Tao. No matter how well-designed our course may look, an experience in nature can teach much more because it evokes the utmost empathy and reverence for every being.

Being a Wu-Wei Teacher

Wu-wei is one of the essential principles of Taoism. Wu-wei translates directly into "non-action." In chapter 48 of *Tao Te Ching*, Lao Tzu said this: "Less and less do you need to force things, until finally you arrive at non-action. When nothing is done, nothing is left undone. True mastery can be gained by letting things go their own way. It can't be gained by interfering."

Wu-wei doesn't imply a passive life attitude towards life; it suggests "action without action, doing without disturbance, or action that does not involve competition or excessive effort" (Yang, Lin, and Culham 2019, 1122). As educators, sometimes we are inundated by *youwei* (action with strong goals). Thus, we bring strong aspirations and ambitions into our classrooms. We expect our students to excel, to succeed, to meet the criteria that we set up for them, without knowing that we are imposing too much pressure on them and disrupting their inner harmony. Every student is like a tree that grows into their unique shape. What we need to do is attentively water them rather than trimming them into the shape that we like. I argue that wu-wei educational philosophy is interpreted as trusting not doubting, listening not interfering, guiding not manipulating, and assisting not dominating. The ultimate objective of wu-wei is to maintain students' naturalness.

There is a famous quote from the *Tao Te Ching*: "The master acts without doing anything and teaches without saying anything" (chapter 2). I realized that good teaching could never be achieved simply by words, so I abandoned the teacher-led mode of instruction. Before the garden club started, I designed several guidelines for the activities: first, the students would have full autonomy to decide what they wanted to delve into. In addition, they would have a chance to experience what they had learned by doing hands-on work since this is the most natural way to learn. The students would also apply the knowledge to solve real-life problems. And most importantly, the whole learning process would be led by students. There wouldn't be any predetermined directions or evaluation criteria.

After our first trip, every student picked out a section of the garden where they would act as guides for the tourists. Each of them consulted a lot of materials to construct their guide scripts. After elaborate preparation and repeated practices on site, they did a quality job in their tour guiding and promoting the garden to a broader audience. In the following several weeks, the staff organized two workshops to demonstrate the process of heritage conservation and restoration. The students had opportunities to engage in practical exercises, such as cleaning the furniture, trimming the plants, and evaluating the wood structures' level of deterioration, under the supervision of the experienced volunteers. Moreover, the students observed the conservation specialists repairing the tilts on the roof of the pavilion and resorting the brick art carvings on the gate, which was a novel experience for them.

Before our field trips, I had raised two questions for the students to investigate: How can we preserve the garden better? How can we engage more young visitors and raise their awareness of heritage protection? We held a small discussion every week after the students finished the volunteer work. Everyone identified the problems they found, including the dangers threatening the garden, the difficulties in preservation, and the inadequacy in promotion. I was amazed by their keen observations. Some students found graffiti on the columns and stones. Another problem raised was that young visitors often glanced through everything hurriedly. One girl noticed that some of the English translation on the explanation boards was inappropriate. Another girl observed the paint peeling off the decorative art pieces. Students also found stone erosion and wood decay at several sites.

I encouraged them to continue observing, to discover the underlying causes of these problems, and develop feasible solutions to these problems. Six weeks later, I was so impressed by their presentations. A group of girls noticed that the products in the garden's souvenir shop were very old fashioned. They mentioned that many museums were launching innovatively designed souvenirs to attract young people. This inspired them to design a series of product models, including eco-bags, mugs, postcards, and phone cases, featuring the garden. They believed that this new marketing strategy could engage more young visitors. The garden management team later took on this suggestion and now visitors can buy various garden-themed creative cultural products in the gift shop. Another impressive group focused on the maintenance of the garden. They found that except for the weather factors, such as rain and wind, which contributed to the decay of the wood architecture, white ants also caused much damage. They took photos of those insect-damaged wood structures and consulted their volunteer supervisors for more advice. They presented their research about the white ants to the management of various Suzhou gardens along with possible countermeasures.

My most pleasant surprise came when the club project was nearing its end. We were visiting the conservation specialists' office, where they were working on restoring a brick carving. They gently brushed off the dust and meticulously applied the paint. A girl suddenly whispered to me: "Olivia, what should I major in if I want to do this job? It's so fascinating!" I looked into her eyes and captured the sparkling curiosity. At that moment, I realized that this club activity might change her life trajectory and direct her to follow her naturalness to become the person she wanted to be. That was the moment when I truly felt a sense of achievement.

Fostering Balance and Harmony in the Classroom

At its base, Taoism is a philosophy about balance. Taoism acknowledges the underlying interconnectedness and interdependence of seemingly opposite things. The opposites blend and complement each other, forming a harmonious unity. Inspired by this philosophy, educators should strive to promote balance in the classrooms by "exploring and making connections" and trying to "move away from fragmentation to connectedness" (Miller 2019a, 16). The balance can be achieved by teaching an interdisciplinary curriculum and offering different types of learning experiences.

During the garden protection project, students gained a sense of balance from participating in different types of learning. Both individual work and collaborative projects were carried out. Additionally, students learned from passive lectures as well as hands-on experience. Besides developing academic skills, they also did physical work like pruning plants. When students investigated the real-life issues of heritage protection, they were actively linking and integrating the knowledge of different subjects. For example, when they examined the difficulties in cultural heritage preservation, they investigated this problem from different angles, including social-economic conditions, historical backgrounds, geographical conditions, natural factors, human activities, and urbanization. It was a good practice for them to learn to look at the world holistically.

Besides taking balanced pedagogical approaches, it is also crucial to maintain a harmonious classroom atmosphere. The classroom atmosphere is like qi in the Taoist way. An impairment of the natural flow of qi will harm a human body. Similarly, an unhealthy classroom atmosphere brings about dysfunctions. Teachers should always be sensitive to the changes of qi in the classroom and nourish the positive qi. One month after our club project started, I detected that the atmosphere was changing in our small community. Before, during the break time, everybody was busy checking social media feeds, until one day, a girl brought a bag of snacks to share. We started to have our routine "tea break." Everyone, including me, brought some snacks and shared them with the others. During this short fifteen minutes, the students talked about school life, family, and dreams. They were not just the schoolmates next door. They were friends now, who shared sorrows and happiness, who cared about each other. The connections between them and me also became closer. Knowing that I was not from Suzhou, they enthusiastically recommended places for me to visit and popular restaurants where I could eat, pouring out how much they loved this city. I also shared with them my stories of growing up. A boy told me that he frequented this garden when he was a small kid because his family used to live only one block away. Their old house was demolished, and his family moved to the new district on the other side of the city. He felt nostalgic every time he was here. At those very moments when we exchanged our stories with genuine feeling, the real harmony was achieved naturally.

Reflection on the Activity

When I recall the memories in the Suzhou garden, the golden foliage of the gingko trees always flashes through my mind. The image reminds me of the young people practising tai chi under the ancient leafy trees in Mount Lao. If I could design the club activity again, I would integrate Taoist contemplative practices into it. The garden was an ideal environment for fostering students' inner peace and tranquility. I would introduce tai chi to my students and practise with them during the breaks, or we could do several minutes' meditation in nature.

The biggest regret that I have about this activity was not paying enough attention to the students' inner world. The final presentation overemphasized students' problem-solving skills instead of their feelings and thoughts about this activity. Although some students actively shared their stories with me, this only happened during the limited break time. I rarely had communication with the introverted students and failed to give enough response to their emotions. If I had the chance to redo this activity, I would invite my students to keep a weekly journal. From these journals, I could understand their deep feelings and give better replies.

Apart from these regrets, I believe this activity sheds some light on applying Taoist teachings into education. Taoism calls for returning to nature, going with the flow, and maintaining one's inner balance. When students were immersed in the garden, they spontaneously reconnected with nature's rhythm and experienced nature's restoring power. During this process, they developed abiding love and respect for every being. In terms of wu-wei philosophy, I hold that we educators need to give autonomy to the students without setting up too many goals or criteria. In my case, this mode of teaching encouraged students to adhere to their naturalness and brought about more authentic learning. Inspired by the teaching of yin-yang balance, I paid attention to the activity design to connect different subjects and offer multiple types of learning experiences. Besides creating a balanced curriculum, we should also not forget to build a genuine relationship with our students, which contributes to a harmonious class atmosphere.

Chapter Two

Bringing Education into Harmony with the Way Things Are

Latter day scholars, not knowing the unity of the Way or the totality of virtue, take up the traces of things that have already happened and sit around talking about them. Even if they are very studious they cannot avoid confusion.

Wen-Tzu (quoted in Cleary 2003c, 178)

How little education has changed. We are still taking up "the trace of things" and ignoring the deeper reality of nature. In our schools and universities, knowledge is broken down into courses, units, lessons, and bits of information. Very little effort is made to show how knowledge and indeed, reality, are interconnected. As a result, children grow up not seeing the interconnectedness of things but instead are caught in the illusion of separateness. They too "cannot avoid the confusion." This illusion underlies seeing people as the "other" which underlies racism and other forms of oppression, so prevalent today.

We need frameworks and methods of teaching and learning that are based on the interconnectedness of life. I have written several books on holistic education as one way to do this. In this book, we explore how Taoism can provide both a broad perspective on teaching and learning as well as some guidelines for how teachers can bring a perspective of interconnectedness into their classrooms. Philosophical Taoism articulates a vision of the universe and life that mirrors the actual realities of nature. This reality is referred to as the Way, the One, or the Tao. Education, teaching, and learning need to be in harmony with the Way if they are to be effective. Central to the Way, and Taoism, is a recognition of how everything is deeply interconnected.

The Tao, or the Way, cannot be easily described in words. Tao is formless and, according to the Sage Lao-Tzu, cannot be named. Still we use words to get some sense of it. Sitting in silent contemplation, a word or phrase can arise that somehow helps in understanding. Or we can get an image that is helpful. These sometimes can be images of nature. For example, in various texts, we see water as a common image of the Tao. In *Tao Te Ching*, Lao-Tzu writes that "water nourishes all things without trying" (chapter 8). Water also changes from rain, to clouds, to snow to ice, and shows how nature is constantly in a state of flux.

Taoism suggests that when we live in harmony with the Way, life flourishes. "Following the nature way brings harmony and prosperity. When the ways of the Tao were followed merchants prospered, farmers reaped good harvest" (Wong 1997, 38). This is an ideal vision of living in harmony with the Tao; however, this vision can also appeal to our desire for wholeness and well-being. There is empirical evidence to support the healthy effects of living according to the Way (Culham and Lin 2020), as well as a number of texts or practice manuals related to "sex, health and long life" (see, for example, Cleary 2003a) and a number of texts related, in part, to topics of "vitality and energy and spirit" (see, for example, Cleary 2003b). When we are one with the Tao, our actions become harmonious with the universe and we can feel the support from the invisible world. Through our intuition we are able to follow the Way, which can bring us to heaven or the celestial realm. Heaven is a state of being where we experience joy since we are part of all that is, the Whole. We are not separate but intimately connected to nature and all beings. "To harmonize with fellow beings is called human joy; to harmonize with the ways of heaven is called celestial joy" (Wong 1997, 147).

When leaders follow the Way, society is peaceful and prosperous; people are not deluded. They work from their centres, the heart, and maintain their connection to the source, the Tao. A Taoist education holds spirit and spirituality at its core (which will be explored later in this book). In the *Wen-Tzu,* Lao-Tzu teaches: "Only spiritual influence is valuable ... The movement caused by a pure heart is like the life-giving influence of the air of spring" (quoted in Cleary 2003c, 176). Virtue is one of the aims of such an education. "Virtue is what you give, not what you get" (201). The *Wen-Tzu* says: "Always keep impartial universal love and do not let it fade. This is called humaneness" (205). Sages do not forget to "help others, day or night; and the extent to which its benefit reaches is far indeed" (180). Virtue or goodness come naturally by staying close to the Way; it does not come from dogma or following some text. "Perfect virtue is uncontrived" (240) and "Ways can be guides, but not fixed paths" (161). In Taoism, there are no ten commandments and eightfold path. Instead, there is simplicity, humility, calmness, and sincerity. These virtues are discussed in the next chapter.

Following Nature

Nature and its ways are the ultimate guide and inspiration to living. In contrast to the effort to control and dominate the natural world in the West, Taoism asks us to trust nature, and ourselves, since we are part of nature. Maria Montessori developed the concept of "cosmic education," which is a good example of an educational approach that emphasizes our place in nature. Cosmic education introduces the child to the universe story and our place in the story. Her son, Mario Montessori (1992), wrote that the child needs to have a "prior interest in the whole" (98) so they can make sense of individual facts. This can be done in part by introducing students to ecological principles that focus on the interdependence of living and non-living things. Mario Montessori gives the example of students studying the life cycle of salmon and its relationship with the environment. Aline Wolf (2004) has also written about Montessori's vision of cosmic education:

> Essentially Montessori's cosmic education gives the child first an all-encompassing sense of the universe with its billions of galaxies. Then it focuses on our galaxy, the Milky Way, our solar system, planet Earth and its geological history, the first specimens of life, all species of plants and animals and finally human beings. Inherent in the whole study is the interconnectedness of all creation, the oneness of things. (6)

Another powerful vision of nature is given by Indigenous Peoples, which can also be introduced to children. One image of the Whole is *Gitchi Manitou* or Great Spirit. I love the work of Richard Wagamese (2016), who writes: "You feel yourself a part of the great wheel of creative, nurturing, loving, benevolent energy that is spinning around us all the time ... I am the trees alive with singing. I am the sky everywhere at once. I am the snow and the wind bearing stories across geographies and generations. I am the light everywhere descending" (30).

Taoism encourages us to trust nature and the cosmos. Alan Watts (1995) argues that nature is "something you must trust; both outside nature – the birds, the bees, the flowers, the mountains, the clouds – but also inside nature, human nature" (30). However, he adds the caveat that "nature is not completely trustworthy" and that is part of "the risk of life" (30). Still, living with trust in ourselves and the cosmos, arguably, is the beginning of deep happiness and joy. This is what Ralph Waldon Emerson (1968) may have felt when he wrote, "In the woods, we return to reason and faith. There I feel that nothing can befall me in life – no disgrace, no calamity (leaving me my eyes), which nature cannot repair" (6).

Learning to trust nature and ourselves is an important step to well-being. Today, many young people suffer from self-doubt and anxiety that can come from social media. Looking to nature provides a powerful antidote and is ever present with the sun, the rain, and the wind. Richard Rohr (2013) has said, "We all somehow believe it is a coherent and even a benevolent universe." He adds that "it is the very heart of the meaning of faith," which is another word for trust (138). From this perspective, we see that life presents us with events and people that help us grow and even thrive. Sometimes these events or people can present great challenges. Indigenous Peoples speak of "Thunder Beings" who enter our lives to test us. I am sure you can think of a Thunder Being in your life.

The Tao and the Whole

The concept of the Tao seems to have become a concept with an apparent universal appeal. On one bookseller's website, I found over fifty titles starting with "The Tao of ..." A small sample:

- *The Tao of Pooh*
- *The Tao of Islam: A Sourcebook on Gender Relationships in Islamic Thought*
- *The Tao of Psychology*
- *The Tao of Money*

- *The Tao of Physics*
- *The Tao of Montessori*
- *The Tao of Watercolor*
- *The Tao of Cooking*

Inevitably, a concept as complex as the Tao is misused in some of these texts; nevertheless, it shows how the *idea* of the Tao has universal appeal for human beings who are looking for an encompassing vision of life and the universe. The ultimate symbol has been given various names such as Brahman, God, logos, the Whole, Great Spirit, Great Mystery, the One, the source of life in all things, and the Tao. The Roman emperor Marcus Aurelius (1997) presented a vision of the relationship between the individual and the whole:

> Whether the universe is a concourse of atoms, or nature is a system, let this first be established: that I am a part of the whole that is governed by nature; next, that I stand in some intimate connection with other kindred parts. For remembering this, inasmuch as I am a part, I shall be discontented with none of the things that are assigned to me out of the whole; for nothing is injurious to the part if it is for the advantage of the whole. (77)

Eckhart Tolle (2005) describes his vision of the Whole: "One the one hand, the whole comprises all that exists. It is the world or the cosmos. But all things in existence, from microbes to human beings to galaxies, are not really separate things or entities, but form part of a web of interconnected multidimensional processes" (276). The Tao gives us a vision of the Whole that is based on nature. It asks us to slow down, breath, and relax into the way things are rather than struggling or fighting reality. This book will explore how this might be done in education.

Meditation Practices

One of the earliest Taoist texts is *Nei-yeh* translated as *Inward Training* (Roth 1999). This text focuses on meditative practices related to the breath and posture and is called "inner cultivation." *Nei-yeh* consists of twenty-six verses, so it is shorter than the *Tao Te Ching*, which has eighty-one chapters. Two verses in *Nei-yeh* mention the One. The 24th verse reads:

1. When you enlarge your mind and let go of it,
2. When you relax your vital breath and expand it,
3. When your body is calm and unmoving:
4. And you can maintain the One and discard the myriad disturbances.
   (Roth 1999, 92)

Here the One, the Way, or the Tao involves meditation, which allows the practitioner to attain the following results:

5. You will see profit and not be enticed by it,
6. You will see harm and not be frightened by it.
7. Relaxed and unwound, yet acutely sensitive,
8. In solitude you delight in your own person.
9. This is called "revolving the vital breath":
10. Your thoughts and deeds seem heavenly. (Roth 1999, 92)

Verse 9 focuses on the One as a place where the person can see the underlying unity of things and, as result, is empowered. In Taoism this empowerment is called *de*. *De* means "virtue" or "power." A person who holds fast to the One will be able to master the myriad of things. Harold Roth (1999) summarizes as follows, "So holding fast to the One entails retaining a sense of a vision of the Way as the one unifying force within phenomenal reality while seeing this reality in all its complexity" (116).

In education it is also important for the teacher to retain a vision of the whole, which includes the whole child and the child's place in the cosmos. Western education with its focus on technique has lost this sense of the One and the Whole. Immersing ourselves in various images of the Whole can help us develop a more inspiring vision of education. Besides Taoism, these include Indigenous visions, as well as visions of universal love provided by Mahatma Gandhi, Martin Luther King Jr., and others, which I discuss in the last chapter.

After discussing the concept of the One, Roth (1999) then has a section entitled "The Holistic Benefits of Inner Cultivation." These include the psychological, spiritual, and physical benefits of the inward training.

The training puts the practitioner in harmony with the universe. These benefits are described in the 16th verse:

1. If people can be aligned and tranquil,
2. Their skin will be ample and smooth,
3. Their ears and eyes will be acute and clear,
4. Their muscles will be supple and their bones will be strong.
5. They will then be able to hold up the Great Circle [of the heavens],
6. And tread firmly over the [Great Square of the earth].
7. They will mirror things with great purity.
8. And will perceive things with great clarity.
9. Reverently be aware [of the Way] and do not waver,
10. And you will daily renew your inner power,
11. Thoroughly understand all under the heavens,
12. And exhaust everything within the Four Directions.
13. To reverently bring forth the effulgence [of the Way]:
14. This is called the "inward attainment."
15. If you do this and but fail to return to it,
16. This will cause a wavering in your vitality. (Roth 1999, 120)

Roth (1999) suggests this is holistic, as the physical benefits are outlined in lines 2 and 4 while the perceptual benefits are in lines 3 and 8, and the psychological benefits are in line 7 with the spiritual benefits in lines 10–12.

The aims of holistic education are similar to this vision. Below are what I believe are the goals of holistic education.

Wholeness/Well-being. The vision of human wholeness is an ancient one as most cultures, including many of those that we now call Indigenous cultures, have some concept of the Whole. Each element in our body is interconnected and our bodies are connected to all that surrounds us. These interconnections form the Whole. Dhayni Ywahoo (1987), a Tsalagi, has written:

> The circle teachings represent the cycle of all things that spiral in the ever-moving universe, in a process of constant movement and subtle change in harmony together. Thus each one of us, within the circle of our own time and space, is every spiraling with our thoughts, words, and actions toward realization of the *whole.* The circle represents complete harmony and balance. (37, my emphasis)

Wholeness recognizes the interconnected nature of experience and the multidimensionality of human beings. Holistic education fosters this awareness in ourselves and in our students. We see the relationship between the physical, intellectual, emotional, and spiritual dimensions of life. Wholeness gives rise to a sense of well-being and happiness. Happiness is not a direct goal of holistic education but can arise when we feel whole and connected. Nel Noddings's (2003) book entitled *Happiness and Education* examines how happiness can be nurtured in educational settings.

Wholeness also includes accepting the "shadow" within. It does not mean creating some ideal model of the human being and trying to live up to that model. Instead, it calls for acceptance for all that happens to us in the moment, which can include suffering, ignorance, and misunderstanding. The tendency in our culture has been to repress our shadow side. Acceptance does not mean glorification of our neuroses, just an awareness that they are there. Lao-Tzu in the *Tao Te Ching* says, "Know the white, yet keep to the black" (chapter 28). This awareness can be the beginning of healing.

Wisdom and Compassion. Wisdom is seeing deeply into the nature of things and acting on that understanding. Science and ecology show the interconnectedness of things, or that everything exists in relationship. When we as human beings *experience* this interconnectedness, a natural compassion can arise for all beings. I emphasize the word *experience* as this is not just an intellectual realization but comes from deep within. Wisdom includes a critical perspective. This is the critical perspective of a Mahatma Gandhi or a Martin Luther King Jr. that sees injustice and acts to resist injustice. However, in the struggle for justice there is still compassion for those who oppose, that is, the oppressors.

Awe and Wonder. Michael Lerner (2000) has stated that awe and wonder should be the first goals of education. Einstein believed that awe and wonder about the mystery of the universe motivated him and other scientists in their inquiries. It is out of this original relationship that awe and wonder naturally manifest. Witnessing nature can give rise to this relationship; for example, watching the clouds move in the sky, seeing a starry night, and observing birds in flight. The arts can also open us to awe and wonder through music, dance, and poetry. William Deresiewicz (2014) emphasizes this by paraphrasing the poet Percy Bysshe Shelley, "art burst the spirit's sleep" (158).

Sense of Purpose/Mastery. Ywahoo (1987) has written, "In the circle of life we each have special gift, a special function ... The gift or function of each person are necessary for the benefit of the whole family of human beings and those that walk, crawl, swim or fly. We are all relatives" (163).

Education should help the student discover what they are good at and how they can commit themselves to working on those gifts or talents. Education should provide spaces for this to happen; a narrow curriculum that focuses on the 3Rs is an obstacle to this discovery. Holistic education should help the student find a sense of purpose in life. Ywahoo (1987) writes how we can discover our life purpose. She says, "Look at what comes easily ... What are the areas you feel called to work in? ... When do you feel the most clear flow of energy?" (104). Of course, we may have more than one life purpose, each of which can change as we grow and develop. So it is important to keep listening within and also hearing what the universe is saying to us.

Conclusion

Taoism and being in harmony with nature can help us realize these goals. We can begin to see how we are part of an interrelated whole that provides the context for teaching and learning. I believe that with the overwhelming challenge of climate change, education should be based on respect for nature and love of the Earth. A Taoist approach to education does this in a way that is life affirming and inclusive. Along with other encompassing visions it can provide a powerful frame for education in the twenty-first century.

The next three chapters discuss some of the major concepts in Taoism – self-cultivation, wu-wei, and yin and yang, and the chapters that follow explore how these concepts can be manifested in practice.

I have relied on four Taoist texts in writing this book: *Chuang-tzu, Nie-yeh, Tao Te Ching,* and *Wen-Tzu.* Who wrote these texts is not clear. Although the *Wen-Tzu* and the *Tao Te Ching* are attributed to Lao-Tzu, very little is known about him. Scholars tend to believe that several people were involved writing these texts who may have been followers of Lao-Tzu. The writings of Alan Watts and Edward Slingerland have also been very helpful.

Chapter Three

Self-Cultivation

Central to Taoism is self-cultivation or self-mastery. It is important for people to master themselves; they need to practise humility and patience. True power comes from self-mastery (Lao-Tzu, *Tao Te Ching*, chapter 33). There are several ways to attain self-cultivation described in Taoist texts.

Silence

One is quietude and silence. Words cannot explain the Way. Taoist texts continually remind us of these words. People who talk do not know, while the wise one keeps silent (Lao-Tzu, *Tao Te Ching*, chapter 56). In *Wen-tzu* we find, "So facial expressions can reach where talk cannot" (Cleary 2003c, 179). I find these lines important since today we are learning more about embodied learning and this understanding was being articulated two thousand years ago. Holistic education recovers and applies the wisdom of the ancients to modern-day issues and concerns.

The implications of this emphasis on silence and embodiment for education are that there should be less stress on verbal communication and the written word. The master teaches without words (Lao-Tzu, *Tao Te Ching*, chapter 43). According to Nakagawa (2002), Aldous Huxley argued that in elementary schools there should be "nonverbal" methods of education used to the develop the whole child. Nakagawa writes that Huxley "presents a unique curriculum, called 'nonverbal humanities,' that embraces diverse methods developed in psychology, psychotherapy, body-mind training, and contemplative traditions" (143). Huxley (1956) defines humans as *homo loquax* (10), or the loquacious one. The result is that language is given priority over immediate experience. He argues that children should be sceptical of language: "Discouraging children from taking words too seriously, teaching them to analyze whatever they hear or read – this is an integral part of the school curriculum" (Huxley 1962, 147). He said education and the nonverbal humanities should help the student "*look at the world directly*" (Huxley 1960, 59, my emphasis). Huxley (1962) also advocated for the use of the Alexander Technique to develop kinesthetic capabilities. Other strategies he suggested included various contemplative practices such as visualization and meditation. In language that echoes today's focus on mindfulness, he argued for "awareness, complete and constant awareness" (quoted in Nakagawa 2002, 157). This awareness, Nakagawa (2002) points out, is "meant to notice that which is taking place in the present moment without any interventions of the mind, such as interpretation, judgment, comparison, etc." (157). Nakagawa links this awareness to "attention," "mindfulness," "witness," or "observation in the contemplative disciplines" (157–8).

Contemplation

"The Embryo of the Tao is formed through the Soft and Gentle Practice of Contemplation. Contemplation allows the person to access the Inner Power," wrote Lao-Tzu in the *Tao Te Ching* (Minford 2018, 313). "Inner Strength is the only True Source of Teaching. It makes Connections. It is an uninterrupted current, one and the same Water, passing from one place to another. It reaches everywhere. The True Gentleman practices the Tao, building Inner Power, Inner Strength, taking every step in a measured way" (312).

This "inner power" is also discussed in the *Nei-yeh* (Roth 1999). It arises through meditation on the breath with an upright sitting posture. The body and limbs need to be aligned so the body is stable, which helps in the development of tranquility. Mindfulness and contemplative education are a growing field today. We can look to Taoism to provide a broad canvas in which we can explore this work. Following the Way involves listening. The *Wen-tzu* describes different levels of listening. First is listening with the ears, then with the mind, and finally the deepest level of listening is with the spirit. Listening involves an emptying and the development of an inner attention, which the person gradually develops over time.

Meditation for the Taoists develops a vital energy, or *qi*, that flows through the body. This qi also flows through the universe and thus connects the person to the cosmos. The *Nei-yeh* (Roth 1999) warns that this energy can dissipate through excessive excitement of the emotions and desires and excessive perception and thought. Excessive thinking and the intellect are dualistic forms of knowing that prevent the person from fully being in harmony with the Way. The goal is to develop the non-dual awareness that resides within. This non-dual awareness is called *shen,* or the "numinous mind," in the *Nei-yeh* (Roth 1999) and is similar to the "celestial mind" found in the *Wen-tzu.* The numinous mind allows the person to fully participate in the Way. Verse 19 in the *Nei-yeh* instructs:

1. By concentrating your vital breath as if numinous,
2. The myriad things will all be contained within you.

The numinous mind contains "the myriad of things," the universe.

My (Jack's) Experience of Teaching Contemplative Practices

Meditation has been part of my life since 1974 when I began *vipassana* or insight meditation. In my teaching at the Ontario Institute for Studies in Education at the University of Toronto, I have required students to do meditation or some form of practice in all my courses since 1988. I believe that doing meditation practice helps my students develop the Inner Power mentioned above. This power or *de* comes through in the presence of the teacher. If we recall the teachers that have had an impact on us, it is not usually the material that they taught that we remember but that elusive quality of presence which somehow touched us.

Teacher presence is often ignored in teacher education as the focus tends to be on theory and teaching strategies; yet it is critically important, particularly in holistic education. Presence and being in the moment mean that there is less chance that we will teach from our egos. If teaching is ego-based, it can become a frustrating series of mini-battles with students. The classroom becomes focused around the issue of control. If we teach from that place where we are present and attentive, teaching can become a more fulfilling and enriching experience. Robert Griffin (1977) summarizes this very well:

> You do not feel set off against them [the students] or competitive with them. You see yourself in students and them in you. You move easily, are more relaxed, and seem less threatening to students. You are less compulsive, less rigid in your thoughts and actions. You are not so tense. You do not seem to be in a grim win-or-lose contest when teaching. (79)

Another important reason for asking students to meditate is that contemplation is a form of self-learning. Through the process of contemplation the person learns to trust one's own deeper intuitive responses. For example, insight meditation is based on the notion that we can learn and grow by simply mindfully watching our own experience. As we notice our own thoughts and agendas, we can gain deeper insight into ourselves and the nature of the mind-body experience. In contrast, the model for most learning at the university level is that the professor and the text are the sources of learning and the student must learn from these external authorities. Contemplation provides one alternative to this model, and recognizes that we can learn from our own direct experience.

A final reason for engaging in contemplation is that it allows teachers to deal with the stresses in their lives. Teaching can be a very stressful profession. Research indicates that meditation is an effective tool in the relaxation process (Smalley and Winston 2010) and given the pressures that teachers face today, this aspect of contemplation should not be overlooked. The vast majority of students in my classes have seen the positive effects of contemplative practice in having fewer headaches and simply being able to address stressful events that come up in their lives and in the classroom. One of my students was a secondary school vice-principal who faced many stressful events during the day. He wrote in his journal that as the pressures of his job increased, he found that he needed to engage in meditation more frequently. Teachers also found that they were less reactive in the classroom.

The Process to Teaching Meditation

After explaining the rationale for engaging in meditation, I first offer a definition of meditation, which is being present in the moment with compassionate awareness. I then introduce the students to eight different types of meditation. We spend approximately two minutes doing each one. I suggest that they choose one to work with for five weeks. These include:

- *Observing the breath.* The student observes the breath, focusing on either the nostrils or the rising and falling of the belly.
- *Counting the breath.* The student counts each exhalation, starting with the first and finishing with the fifth exhalation. In both these breath exercises, I note that the student should not try to control the process but breathe naturally.
- *Body scan.* The student mindfully scans the body from head to foot and then foot to head.
- *Mantra.* A sound or phrase is repeated silently.
- *Visualization.* The student visualizes a series of images, usually from an experience in nature.
- *Walking.* This practice focuses the awareness on the foot leaving and touching the ground.
- *Passage.* The student selects a short passage of poetry or inspirational text and repeats it silently.
- *Loving-kindness.* Thoughts of well-being are sent first to ourselves and then to others.

If the student already has a practice, I do not ask them to change what they are doing. Students are asked to start meditating 5 to 10 minutes a day and over the course of five weeks gradually work up to 20 or 30 minutes. Some students are able to begin with 20 minutes a day. They a keep a daily journal describing how the process is going and they are asked to report on what the body is experiencing during the meditation and what was prominent during the practice (e.g., thoughts, sounds). Here is one example of a daily entry:

> Aug. 2nd
> **Observing the breath**
> Profoundly noticeable a number of times during this session was the wave of relaxation moving thought my legs from top to bottom. I could feel the tension leaving the body, flowing out through the tips of my toes. Other thoughts came and went as I attempted to return to the breathing and the awareness of my chest moving up and down. My hands melted into my knees. I felt rejuvenated and ready for the rest of the evening.

I encourage students also to submit questions to me in their journals if any issues arise during their practice. At the end of the five weeks they write a one- or two-page summary reflection on their practice. Here are the reflections of one woman that also include how she brought her practice into her teaching:

> Through daily meditation, I have been able to take some time for myself in order to relax, regain a sense of who I am and my physical needs. I have taken the opportunity to meditate daily for the past six weeks (and counting) in order to take into consideration the simple things that I can do for myself to help myself feel better, such as breathing properly and taking time to really enjoy little things that I experience, as opposed to moving on to the next thing without appreciating what I've just seen or felt.
>
> I found that the energy that was generated from my meditative experience stayed with me for much of the day. I have felt great over these past couple of months and have attributed that much of that to the feeling of comfort with myself and a positive outlook on things. I really have felt that meditation has had an impact on my relationships with others. My attention seemed more focused at work and in my personal life following meditation.
>
> The relationship that I have had with my class has been a close one, yet I feel that our class meditations have brought many of us much closer. My students write journal entries about finding their "star" and going to their "garden" as they meditate on their own at home (often at bedtime as they begin their dreams!). One seven-year-old student's reflection that really stands out to me is

that: "meditation makes me feel kind of in between" not happy or sad, "just calm." This, with the added energy and an overall sense of satisfaction with life, seemed to sum it up for me, too.

The student's comment on just being calm has a Taoist ring to it as calmness is one of the central virtues of Taoism.

A student in another class wrote about her experiences of being sexually abused:

Daily practice has taught me that there is nothing I need to do, fix, or control in my life. Perfection, wholeness, and completion are always with me. I feel this almost as soon as I settle into my practice. Deep feelings of what I can only describe as security and comfort engulf me. Meditation requires me to sit with myself, alone and without distractions. At times this is challenging, especially as an individual dealing with PTSD, when memories and thoughts arise that elicit highly emotional responses. However, in general, I have found myself experiencing fewer flashbacks and when they do occur, I am able to detach myself from them. I no longer fully identify with "my story" and "what happened to me" as meditation has helped me become acquainted to a deeper part of myself, one that cannot be altered or harmed, a part of me that is divine. I have come to understand that loving awareness is my natural state of being. As I explore a new way of being alone and intimate with myself, a new sense of closeness to my inner nature is continuously revealed.

Some of themes that run through the students' journals include:

- Giving permission to be alone and enjoy their own company;
- Increased listening capacities;
- Feeling increased energy;
- Being less reactive to situations and generally experiencing greater calm and clarity.

There are two other elements that are included in my classes. I begin each class with the loving-kindness meditation. The essence of this meditation is to centre ourselves in the heart area and to contact a basic warmth there. After connecting with the heart, we then attempt to share this warmth and energy with others. There are various forms of loving-kindness and the one below was taught to me by a Burmese monk, U Silananda. I have made some minor changes in the wording.

> May I be well, happy, and peaceful.
> May my family be well, happy, and peaceful.
> May my friends be well, happy, and peaceful.
> May my neighbours be well, happy, and peaceful.
> May my colleagues be well, happy, and peaceful.
> May all people that I meet be well, happy, and peaceful.
> May all people that I am having difficulty or feel anger towards be well, happy, and peaceful.
> May all beings on this planet be well, happy, and peaceful.
> May all beings in this universe be well, happy, and peaceful.

This approach starts with those who are emotionally closest to us and then moves out from there. Another approach is to move out geographically. Such as:

> May I be well, happy, and peaceful.
> May all beings in this room be well, happy, and peaceful.
> May all beings in this building be well, happy, and peaceful.
> May all beings in this neighbourhood be well, happy, and peaceful.
> May all beings in this town or city be well, happy, and peaceful.
> May all beings in this region be well, happy, and peaceful.
> May all beings in this planet be well, happy, and peaceful.
> May all beings in this universe be well, happy, and peaceful.

When you are doing the loving-kindness, it is also possible to visualize the people that you are sending these thoughts to. One student shared her experience of the loving-kindness practice:

> I had another visualization experience that I would like to share as I did in my last journal submission. I am not sure why such visualizations come to me when our class engages with the Love and Kindness meditation, however, I am grateful for these experiences I see so vividly in my mind. As I closed my eyes and settled into my seat, I was ready to begin my breaths.

As Jack usually starts his Love and Kindness meditation with the self, Jack recited, "May I be well, happy and peaceful." Instantaneously, I envisioned this shining bright light illuminating my heart. It was a soft, yellow-white light that floated so gracefully near my heart. When I saw this glow, I thought perhaps this was my soul, but I wasn't quite sure. Whatever it was made me feel warm, happy and calm deeply inside. As Jack went on with this meditation, I envisioned this light shining through every single person in our class as we spread the love to those around us. As we wished people around OISE to be well, happy and peaceful, I visualized myself walking throughout the building and seeing people walking by with their glowing hearts shining bright. As our love spread to those within the provincial level, I saw people from various places I've been before with illuminating hearts. When we reached the level of all beings, I imagined a radiant glowing planet full of billions of tiny bright lights radiating into the universe. This vision was absolutely breathtaking. How a simple mediation instantaneously brought my mood up to a more happy and positive state was truly remarkable and eye-opening. After this experience, I am strongly considering adding the Love and Kindness meditation into my future practices.

I start my classes with this exercise and I find that it has added immeasurably to the tone and feel of the class. Research is now beginning on loving-kindness practice. It was found in one study that university students who were taught this practice that their kindness increased among them compared to a control group where the imagery was neutral (Hutcherson, Seppala, and Gross 2008).

Here is a beautiful statement about love in the *Wen-tzu*, "Even the ignorant do not harm those they love. If you could truly have all people in the world embosom a heart of human love, where would calamity come from? ... Accumulated love becomes good fortune, accumulated hatred becomes calamity" (quoted in Cleary 2003c, 213, 232).

The third element that I include is introducing the students to mindfulness practice in daily life. This means being attentive and present to activities during the day. I encourage them to start with one daily activity (e.g., doing the dishes, preparing a meal, brushing their teeth) and to do it without thinking about something else. Beginning with simple daily tasks can build a foundation of mindfulness that can eventually extend to the classroom so that teachers can be more present to their students. One former student describes her mindfulness experiences: "I find these little moments kind of funny when they happen because all of a sudden I become very aware that I'm washing the dishes or vacuuming ... And I kind of get into the moment, and it stays with me during the day."

Another student, Astrid, teaches in an elementary school. Here is how she integrates mindfulness practice into her day of teaching:

> I began each day marveling at the miracle of life, of falling asleep and awakening to a wondrous world. With this thought, I began my morning rituals. Thinking of my daily routines as rituals actually helped me in attaining a more aware state as I washed my face, took my shower, ate my breakfast and walked (or drove) to work. Upon entering the school, I decided to go to my classroom first. I had previously been going into the office to sign in and say good morning, etc. but this took away from the oneness that I needed in my "mindfulness" training. I ritualized all my tasks – walking up the stairs, putting the key into the classroom door, hanging up my coat etc. It was actually amazing how being mindful of these simple tasks allowed me to begin my day in a calm, clear and less cluttered way. How many times had I come into this room, dumped my coat, hat and mitts on my chair, ran to the photocopy room and back, spent another half hour looking for the photocopying I had laid down somewhere, not to mention the frantic search for mitts when it was time go out on duty? Instead, I began to become aware of my mornings in the classroom and in turn they became calm and focused.
>
> My most favorite part of this pre-school ritual is writing the schedule on the board. My team teacher had tried to talk me out of this last June (she writes the daily schedule for each day on the sheets of chart paper and laminates them). At the time, I explained to her that writing of the schedule on the board had many different purposes for me. The most important one was that it allowed me to center myself in the classroom. I look back now on how intuitive I had been and I am amazed. Being mindful of this particular ritual has made me fully aware of the "here" during the hectic day. I stand at the front of the room and feel the smooth texture of the chalk in my hands. I think about where I am and I observe my surroundings – the plants, the books, the desks, the children's slippers – I am, for the second time that day, amazed at the miracle of life.

The day begins, I stand outside the classroom fully aware of each individual as they enter the room. I interact with them, I say hello; it feels good. This is new, until now, I had never made it to the door when the children entered – I was always too busy! I try to maintain this sense of awareness – aware of my feelings (physical and emotional) and my reactions to the things that are happening "now." Of course, the craziness of the classroom day begins and it becomes more and more difficult to maintain this awareness as the day wears on. However, now instead of working through recess, I take the time to visit with colleagues in the staff room. When I can, I take a walk down to the beach at lunch and look out across the lake, mindful of the beauty of the world around me. When the day ends, I recapture this mindful state and fully participate in the end-of-day ritual with my students. After the children have left, I sweep the floor, being mindful of my movements and the sound of the broom. I often begin by thinking that I am sweeping the day's events away and that I am focusing on the "now" – the actual act of sweeping. The pleasure of being here, and being able to fully participate reminds me again of the miracle of life. (quoted in Miller 2006, 79–80)

The students in my graduate classes are mostly teachers working in public or Catholic schools. About 70 to 80 per cent are women and the ages range from the mid-twenties to the fifties. Toronto has been identified as one of the most multicultural cities in the world and my classes reflect that diversity. Students from Brazil, China, Egypt, Indonesia, Iran, Italy, Jamaica, Japan, Kenya, Korea, Lebanon, Malta, Serbia, Tibet, Ukraine, and Vietnam have been in my classes. The average class size is around twenty-four students. To date, more than two thousand students have been introduced to meditation practice in these courses. So far, there has not been one student who has reported an overall negative experience with the practice during the course.

Calmness

Calmness is a virtue in Taoism. Eva Wong (2015) writes, "If you are able to still your thoughts and maintain peace and simplicity, the Tao will emerge within" (100). In my research on the effects of meditation, I found this was one of the qualities that arose from meditation practice (Miller and Nozawa 2002). One female nursing instructor commented: "I'm not as agitated … or I'm not as arousable from the point of view that things don't bother me as much … I feel calmer, I feel more … this word centered keeps coming to mind."

One principal commented how calmness is important to the whole process of change, "And to get any kind of change happening in schools, it's imperative that people are calm and are in an almost meditative state in order to make those changes that are being demanded." This principal ran meetings that didn't have an agenda: "We're just here to talk about the work that we're doing, and enjoy each other." She adds this is "not team building, it's just kind of being together, it doesn't have a name." Her approach is an example of the benefits of not over planning or calculating. In Taoism, calculation or contrivance are not congruent with the Way. "The Way of Nature is spoiled by those who contrive, lost by those who grasp … Those who let calculation run their lives, work hard without accomplishment" (*Wen-tzu*, quoted in Cleary 2003c, 273, 166).

A related effect is that the participants commented that they are not as reactive with students as they step back from troublesome situations. A female teacher noted: "You can get really frustrated with these kids because these kids get really angry and frustrated because they can't read, and your first response is to be an authoritarian, when actuality they just need to be hugged and loved. So it (the meditation) really helps me to step back and look at what really is going on." Another teacher simply said, "I don't remember the last time I raised my voice." She added that one of her students told her, "Miss, how come you're so calm all the time?"

Sincerity and Self-Cultivation

"The Spirit of the Thing Itself tells you that there is more to be had and so you must continue to ask of it to reveal ever more. And because you are sincere in your heart it will. That is the nature of Heaven" (Stephen Kaufman 1998, 74). In referring to the sages, Lao-Tzu says, "Even if they don't say a single word, nevertheless all the people in the world, the birds and beasts, the ghosts and spirits, evolve along with them" (*Wen-tzu*, quoted in Cleary 2003c, 176).

To be in harmony with the Way, our intention should be clear. Clear intention brings this sincerity. There should be no thought of reward, just the sincere effort to be in harmony with how things are. This is similar to "right effort" or "right resolve" in the Eightfold Path of Buddhism. Perhaps the best example of this sincerity was found in Mahatma Gandhi. He held no political office, but his total commitment to non-violence was unquestioned and touched not only his fellow citizens in India but also many others around the world.

In teaching, the teacher's presence should reflect this sincerity. Most of us have had the privilege of having one teacher in our life that was truly present. John Makransky (2007), a Buddhist scholar, describes the presence of one of his teachers, Geshe Tsering:

> While studying and engaging in philosophical debates with him, he treated me with such gentle respect and love that, when I reluctantly left at the end of the day, I felt like a different person. Something was awakened in me by his presence, a deep desire to be like him and a recognition that somehow, mysteriously, I could. It made me grateful to be alive. (147)

Makransky says the teachings flowed from Tsering's "whole manner of being. He was a remarkable teacher, whose effectiveness flowed from his unwavering and unconditional love for all whom he served" (147).

John O'Donohue's (1999) writings about presence are also worth considering:

> Presence is the whole atmosphere of a person or thing ... Presence has a depth that lives behind the form or below the surface. There is a well of presence within everything hidden from the human eye. This comes in different ripples to the surface. No two stages of presence are ever exactly the same. The flow of soul within means the surface is always different. (53–4)

Although attentiveness is at the core of presence there is also a mysterious element – the soul. O'Donohue talks about charismatic presence which is rooted in self-belonging. He writes, "It is the art of belonging to one's soul that keeps one's presence aflame" (66). O'Donohue believes this anchoring of presence in soul leads to dignity and beauty. With this dignity there is "no forcing of presence," these people "do not drive themselves outwards to impress" (68). O'Donohue's conception of presence contains the notion of not forcing or not trying but something that can flow naturally. This is similar to the Taoist concept of wu-wei, which will be discussed in the next chapter.

Non-violence and Embracing the Feminine

Taoism rejects the use of force. Wong (2015) writes:

> … The Sage lives in accordance with the Tao, abides in nonaction, and keeps her energy in harmony and balance. She cultivates humility and softness and abstains from the use of force.
> … The Sage wins respect through humility … He values the feminine; therefore he can live forever. (112)

Gandhi was an example of embracing the feminine. He once said, "I have counted myself as a woman" (quoted in R. Gandhi 2008, 518).

> Those around Gandhi did not tend to look at him as either male or female. In his search for the full realization of his human nature he became a balanced blend of both masculine and feminine qualities. In fact, one of his nieces, Manubhen, wrote a short book about her time with her famous uncle called, "Bapu, My Mother." "Bapu," interestingly enough, means "father"; but he was less like a father or an uncle to her than a nurturing parent, embodying both Father and Mother. (Van Hook 2015)

Another person who included the feminine was Fred Rogers and his television show for children, *Mr. Rogers' Neighborhood*. The show was unlike so many other shows for children as it was slow paced and focused on feelings. For example, Rogers did shows that explored issues such as divorce and death. In a recent biography, his work was described as including a "surprising amount of information and cognitive learning but did so in ways that were always processing opportunities for social and emotional learning as well" (King 2018, 209). It has been said that Fred Rogers reached more children than any teacher ever, and his work could be called holistic because he focused on the child's emotional well-being as well as their cognitive development. His work was also deeply spiritual. Although he was Christian, his approach was eclectic and focused on compassion and kindness as central values.

Rogers was not unlike the ancient Sages that are referred to in the Taoist literature. In the *Wen-tzu*, it reads, "They (the Sages) nurture the people fairly; authority is not commanding, the legal system is not complicated, *education is spiritual*" (quoted in Cleary 2003c, 174, my emphasis). The concept of yin also is symbolic of the feminine and interacts with yang to create wholeness. The concepts of yin and yang are explored in chapter 5.

Humility

Humility is another central virtue in Taoism. As a person sees himself or herself as part of nature, it brings a natural humility. "Being still within permits a man to express himself fully without having to avoid the limitations imposed by his attempting to think of a higher reality. This is why you should be humble before Heaven. This is why you should express humility beneath the power of Heaven" (Kaufman 1998, 34).

We live in the day of self-promotion and celebrity worship. The ego is out of control as narcissism rules. Humility can be seen as weakness. It is important to root the humility in nature so that it is not false or contrived. If we use nature as a guide, then it helps bring about this kind of humility.

As teachers we realize that learning never ends. We are constantly curious about the world, our subject matter, and how children learn. Our curiosity should match the curiosity of the child. Through this curiosity we can see ourselves in the students. Sometimes when we take on a major learning project (e.g., learning a new language), we can feel how the students must feel in learning something new and difficult. This curiosity keeps us humble; we realize there is never an end to the learning process.

We are also humbled by the fact that we can never fully know the results of our teaching. Sometimes we will hear from a student years after they were in our class about how much they learned from us. Yet these are isolated incidents and we can wonder about our effect on all the other students we worked with over the years. Clearly, there is a mystery to teaching and being aware of this mystery is truly humbling. Henry Adams wrote, "A teacher affects eternity; he can never tell where his influence stops" (quoted in Howe 2003, 238).

Tom Culham (2013) writes about the relationship between contemplation and the connection to the Taoist virtues, particularly the virtue of tranquility with reference to *Nei-ye*. He writes about inner-cultivation and how contemplation supports the development of tranquility and awareness (82–3).

Conclusion

Self-cultivation should be the goal for both teachers and students, and it needs to start with the teacher. If they are going to introduce any form of contemplation into the classroom, teachers need to be doing their own practice. Again, I cite Minford's (2018) commentary on the *Tao Te Ching*:

> Inner Strength is the only True Source of Teaching. It makes Connections. It is an uninterrupted current, one and the same Water, passing from one place to another. It reaches everywhere. The True Gentleman practices the Tao, building Inner Power, Inner Strength, taking every step in a measured way. (312)

This is my experience as a teacher. My own practice has been my source, and I believe it has helped me make connections with my students. All the practices and virtues discussed here as ways to develop self-cultivation can help us align ourselves with the Way of things. As we gain understanding through experience, the virtues arise naturally in our life rather than being forced.

Wong's (2015) translation of *Chuang-Tzu*, summarizes the Taoist approach to living and learning, which beautifully summarizes the ideas presented in this chapter:

> Discarding flowery knowledge, doing away with the importance of self, not forcing your will on others, and not meddling with the natural course of things are the principles of the way. Don't be too serious and pedantic, but at the same time don't be too cavalier. Take out the corners and file down the rough edges so that you can tumble and turn with the ten thousand things. Go beyond acceptance

and rejection. Don't get stuck on what came before, and don't be anxious over what will come afterward, but rest in the immediacy of the present … If you rest in stillness, you will never lose clarity and good judgment … When you are not preoccupied with yourself, then things will reveal their true nature to you. Let your movement be as fluid as water, your stillness like that of a mirror … Where others tire their bodies and minds for achievement and profit, be easy going and leisurely. Use profundity as your root and simplicity as your guide. (192)

Chapter Four

Wu-Wei: Teaching with Ease and Grace

Wu-wei is usually translated as non-doing or not trying. It is a concept foreign to Western thinking as we live in a culture of doing and achieving. At its core, wu-wei is a way of being in the world. Edward Slingerland (2014) has written about wu-wei in his book *Trying Not to Try: The Art and Science of Spontaneity.* Here is his description of wu-wei:

> It refers to the dynamic, effortless, and unselfconscious state of mind of a person who is optimally active and effective. People in *wu-wei* feel as if they are doing nothing, while at the same time they might be creating a brilliant work of art, smoothly negotiating a complex social situation, or even bringing the entire world into harmonious order. For a person in *wu-wei*, proper and effective conduct follows as automatically as the body gives in to the seductive rhythm of a song. This state of harmony is both complex and holistic, involving as it does the integration of the body, the emotions and the mind. (7)

Slingerland refers to research on cognition to explain wu-wei. He makes the distinction between conscious, rational thought (which he calls cold cognition) and unconscious, embodied knowing (which he terms hot cognition). The aim of wu-wei is to have both cold and hot cognition work together. Slingerland writes, "For a person in *wu-wei*, the mind is embodied and the body is mindful; the two systems-hot and cold, fast and slow – are completely integrated. The result is an intelligent spontaneity that is perfectly calibrated to the environment" (29).

Chuang-Tzu gives the example of the butcher, Ding, and how he slices the ox:

When I first began cutting up oxen, all I could see was the ox itself. After three years, I no longer saw the ox as a whole. And now I meet it with my spirit and don't look with my eyes. My senses and conscious awareness have shut down and my spiritual desires take me away. I follow the Heavenly pattern of the ox, thrusting into the big hollows, guiding the knife through the big openings, and adapting my motions to the fixed structure of the ox. In this way, I never touch the smallest ligament or tendon, much less a main joint. (quoted in Watson 1968, 51)

Ding goes on to say that he is able to "to pass through gaps where there is space" and thus the edge of the blade does not need sharpening. Slingerland (2014) points out that this is a metaphor for living as the "*wu-wei* person moves only through the open spaces in life avoiding the difficulties that damage one's spirit and wear out one's body" (21).

For the teacher, it is also seeing the spaces that allow for learning and connection. However, education and teaching tend to be dominated by rational, logical thinking or cold cognition. Cold cognition tends to be calculating and can lead to mistrust while hot cognition, because it is spontaneous, leads to acceptance and trust. Slingerland (2014) argues that we overlook the latter. He translates wu-wei as "effortless action" or "spontaneous action." He writes that wu-wei is "relaxing and enjoyable in a deeply rewarding way" (8). People who have this quality exhibit what the Taoists called *de*, which I discussed in the previous chapter. De means virtue or power that arises through being in harmony with the Way. Slingerland (2014) asserts, "If you have *de*, people like you, trust you, and are relaxed around you" (8). Trust and relaxation are important qualities for teachers as well, so wu-wei and de are explored in this chapter in more detail. Slingerland links wu-wei to Csikszentmihalyi's (1990) concept of "flow," although he points out differences between the two concepts. Wu-wei involves being connected to something larger than ourselves, the Tao, or the Way. Slingerland (2014) argues that this makes it different from flow, which does not have this larger context that also includes a sense of the sacred. I also believe there are similarities between wu-wei and grace as described by Sarah Kaufman (2016), which also is explored in this chapter.

Slingerland (2014) argues that spontaneity as described by the early Chinese is a "cornerstone of individual well-being and human sociality" (18). The Western focus on the rational, logical approach to living and problem solving is dysfunctional and contributes to unhappiness and frustration. I believe this is also true in education, which has often adopted rational approaches to improvement and change. I agree with Slingerland, who writes, "The goal of education should not be to teach people logic and self-control but rather to guide them in nurturing a set of positive, innate tendencies into full *wu-wei* dispositions" (115).

Wu-Wei and Tzu-Jan

Chuang-Tzu or Chuang Tsu, wrote about wu-wei in a manner that we can understand. As well as the example of the butcher, another comes from archery. Eugen Herrigel studied archery in Japan under a master. His master's advice was that he be "absolutely self-oblivious and without purpose ... You must act as if the goal were infinitely far off" (Herrigel 1971, 58, 62). He goes on to say, "There are processes which are beyond the reach of understanding ... The spider dances her web without knowing there are flies that will get caught in it ... So, too, the archer hits the target without having aimed – more I cannot say" (64–5).

Closely connected to the concept of wu-wei is *ziran,* or *tzu-jan,* which can be translated as spontaneity. Tzu-jan is seen as inherent in the human being and arises when the ego is absent and the person is connected with the surrounding environment. Ray Grigg (1994) writes that tzu-jan is "grounded within the circle of direct experience, connected to it but not oppressed by it" (298). The beating of our heart and our breathing just go on of their own accord without conscious effort. This natural state arises in animals and in human beings when they act from the embodied unconscious that Slingerland (2014) refers to. In Zen there is phrase that when we sit, we just sit, and when we walk, we just walk. Shunryu Suzuki (1973) writes, "When we forget ourselves, we actually are the true activity of the big existence, or reality itself. When we realize this fact there is no problem whatsoever in the world, and we can enjoy our life without feeling any difficulties" (73). Grigg (1994) summarizes:

> When people are naturally themselves, when they are unfashioned by any preconception about what they ought or ought not to be, and who they might or might not be, they inadvertently become one with the wholeness of things. This

does not make them "perfect" according to some narrow system of idealistic judgment. But it does give them an integrity of being that intuitively and spontaneously follows a wisdom that is greater than themselves. (301)

Ding, the butcher, describe three stages in developing wu-wei. First, he sees the whole ox. Then he sees the various parts. At the third stage his senses shut down and "my spiritual desires take me away" and follow the wisdom that Grigg refers to. At this third stage, wu-wei and embodied knowing allow the butcher to work without conscious effort and, instead, he acts in accordance with Heaven. The Way and the Chinese idea of Heaven are connected. Heaven is not a place but, like the Way, is the ultimate source of goodness. Because of this connection, action is part of a greater whole, "it is this holistic, social, and religious quality of *wu-wei* that makes it unique" (Slingerland 2014, 42). Wu-wei is not confined to the individual but includes that larger holistic and sacred context.

In contrast, Csikszentmihalyi's (1990) concept of flow does not include this holistic, social, and religious quality. It focuses on individual challenge and spiralling complexity. Slingerland (2014), however, writes about a person, Serafina Vinon, described in Csikszentmihalyi's (1990) work, who manifests wu-wei. She is seventy-one years old and works on a farm in the Swiss Alps. Her life is not easy on the farm, but she enjoys the outdoors and the animals. Nature and her culture provide the larger whole of which she is a part. As described in the chapter 1 of this book, Nature with a capital "N" is a guide to living a Taoist life and helps nurture wu-wei.

Slingerland (2014) says that "the distinguishing feature of *wu-wei* is the absorption of the self into something greater" (47). This connection often involves a sense of the "sacred" that brings a sense of gratitude. It also may include ritual or activities that involve movement that develop the embodiment of wu-wei. One can sense the Tao and feel its support. Wu-wei allows us to relax into the Way. Contemplative practices described in the last chapter help to develop our intuitive sense of the Way. Tai-chi, qi-qong and yoga also can nourish this connection. In Chuang Tsu (1974), Wang Ni describes when this connection is very strong:

The perfect man is spiritual. Though the great swamp burns, he will not feel the heat. Though the great rivers freeze, he will not feel the cold. Though thunderbolts split the mountains and gales shake the sea, he will have no fear. Such a man can ride the clouds and mist, mount the sun and moon, and wander beyond the four seas. Life and death do not affect him. (40)

Master Chang Wu Tsu adds,

Ordinary men labor and toil. The sage acts without choosing. He experiences then thousand years in one age. To him the ten thousand things are what they are, yet they form one whole. (42)

We may not "ride on the energy of the clouds," but we can experience what Serafina does in feeling in harmony with Nature and how things are. If this sense is deeply rooted in our being, then our students will feel it as well. This leads to de and the trust that arise from that. De is seen by Makransky (2007) in his teacher, Geshe Tsering: "Something was awakened in me by his presence, a deep desire to be like him and a recognition that somehow, mysteriously, I could. It made me grateful to be alive" (147).

Ways to Cultivate Wu-Wei and Tzu-Jan

There is not one way to develop wei-wu and tzu-jan. Slingerland (2014) continually points out the tension in Taoism that doing meditation or any other practice is a form of trying. Chuang-Tzu seems to support two approaches to achieving wu-wei; the sudden one where it appears without effort, and the other one that is more of a Confucian type that is gradual and involves some form of practice or instruction. Paradox is inherent in Taoism and certainly in trying not to try. Herrigel (1971) wrote, "Must I become purposeless-on purpose?" (35). Chuang-Tzu uses stories to present various paradoxes, and often this is done to deliberately confuse readers to set them off balance. Similar to the Zen koan, these stories can sometimes lead to sudden awakening.

As Slingerland (2014) describes, Ancient Chinese teachers offered different paths. He starts with Confucius, who advocated studying classic texts such as the *Book of Odes* with other students under the guidance of a teacher. The Confucian approach is not usually associated with Taoism, but Slingerland makes the case that this more traditional approach has its place in developing wu-wei. He refers to recent psychological research on the cognitive science of ritual for support. One aspect of the Confucian approach was music and singing. The *Book of Odes* contained folk songs that people sang during their work in the fields. Singing these songs and dancing helps the person connect to the unconscious or hot cognition. Singing and dancing in a group can bring *ec-stasis*, or ecstasy, and can help the person make the "transition from disciplined self-control to spontaneous, but properly ordered, joy in the Way" (76).

In her book *The Lost Art of Scripture*, Karen Armstrong (2019) writes about ancient Chinese practices and also emphasizes the importance of ritual and bodily movement. She writes, that a "skillfully devised rite can also yield transcendent experience in which the participant goes beyond the self in an *ekstasis* and experiences a profound transformation" (81). These practices were to help the development of *shu*, or reciprocity, and *ren*, or empathy and compassion. The Chinese Confucian philosopher Xunzi describes the process, "The learning of the gentleman enters his ear, becomes firm in his heart-mind, spreads out through his four limbs and manifests itself in both activity and repose. In his merest word, in his slightest movement, the gentleman can always be taken as an example and a model" (Knoblock 1990, 76).

Grace

This description of a gentleman is not dissimilar from Sarah Kaufman's (2016) concept of grace. She describes grace in a manner similar to wu-wei, as grace involves "the mind, the disciplined body, and, most especially the understanding heart" (xxii). She also says that grace is "the unexpected glimmering thing that happens, so subtle that no one else might notice … But the impact is real and deep" (27). Her description of manner has a Confucian tone as grace should foster "harmonious interactions" and create "a climate of warmth and appreciation" (48). Kaufman quotes Elizabeth Woodward (1935) who wrote that grace is about "how you carry yourself every day," which begins with a still mind (57). Grace is also "about ease that comes from self-control" (61). Kaufman also refers to the Italian concept of *Sprezzatura*, which "meant avoiding affectation while also making whatever is done or said appear to be without *effort*" (65, my emphasis).

Kaufman (2016) gives examples of grace from different areas such as the arts, sports, and even politics. As in meditation and movement, body posture and walking are signifiers of grace. "A graceful walk brings the body into natural balance. The weight glides forward and over solid footing. There is power in the midsection and buoyancy in the upper body" (168). Good posture is "comfortable, balanced and fluid." Kaufman asserts that like de, "grace inspires trust" (168). One of my students described how posture and walking were a way of centring herself:

> For teachers, there are important behaviours to be mindfully considered: body language, eye contact, and compassionate speech. As I walk down the hall from my office where I have been handling administrative duties to my classroom where I want to shift my focus to my students, I try to pay attention to my walk – my posture, my speed, my gait. I relax the muscles in my face and put on a smile. Sometimes that smile comes more naturally than at other times but the result is always the same – my mood shifts and I become less defensive and more receptive. I start each class with erect posture, looking forward and ready to meet the students. I think my body language has a strong positive impact to the start of each class.
>
> Eye contact is an extension of body language and a very real and immediate way to focus on the students. I try to make eye contact with every student as I walk through the class. They are usually engaged in a variety of activities and conversations but my eye contact and my close physical proximity to each student allow them to refocus on our class and we connect with each other. (Miller 2014, 151)

A graceful classroom is one that is relaxed, yet there is also an energy. Slingerland (2014) writes about the connection between wu-wei and de and states that they lead to an "easy oneness with things, a state of going along with whatever presents itself, which no expectations and calculation. Such perfect relaxation brings with it incredible efficacy in the world" (102). Of course, it is a challenge to have a classroom with such ease and efficacy, but it is a certainly a worthy goal that would make teaching and learning more enjoyable and effective.

Like wu-wei, grace helps in connecting people to something larger than themselves. "The most meaningful application of grace is to connect us more deeply with one another (or perhaps especially?) in the smallest moments" (Kaufman 2016, 207). Grace is being aware of others and responding to them in helpful ways. This includes simple acts such as holding the door open for another or giving up one's seat on a crowded subway. The teacher just cited above describes how mindfulness helps her respond to students in the classroom:

> Being mindful in our classrooms we are able to slow our thoughts and actions and become aware of our students' needs, see how we are meeting them, and how the students are affected and respond to our actions ... When we teach mindfully, we know what we are teaching. We are aware of the words we speak, the tone in which we speak them, we are able to deeply observe and listen to our students and aware of connectedness between student and teacher and indeed all the members of the classroom community. We are able to see the presentation of the curriculum and adjust it to the situation. (Miller 2014, 151)

Kaufman (2016) refers to Scott Perlo, the associate director of Jewish programming at Sixth & I, a historic Washington synagogue, who said, "Grace is quality that inspires love." He adds that it is an intangible quality that is "very difficult to define and adds a special quality to your actions" (246).

At the end of her book, Kaufman (2016) finishes with guides to living life gracefully:

- Slow down. There is no way to be graceful when you're rushing around haphazardly.
- Practice tolerance and compassion. This goes along with slowing down. Take time to listen and understand.
- Make room for others – on the sidewalk, at the bus stop, in a coffee shop, during a business meeting, and in your life.
- Strive to make things easy for people, even in small ways.
- Make things easy for yourself. Be easily pleased. Accept compliments, take a seat on the bus if someone offers it to you, embrace kindness that comes your way. This is graciousness and it is a gift for someone else. You are giving another person the gift of being graceful.
- Lighten your load. Shed painful shoes, disencumber yourself of heavy purses, backpacks, and briefcases. Let the bad stuff go, physically and emotionally.

- Take care of your body. The more you move, the better you'll move. And the better you'll feel.
- Be generous. It's a lovely thing to anticipate and fulfil someone's hopes.
- Enjoy. Raise a glass, as Lionel Barrymore did in the movie *Grand Hotel*, "to our magnificent, brief, dangerous life – and the courage to live it." (277–8)

It is possible to see this list as counter to the idea of wu-wei, and this is certainly the case if one forces these activities or takes a mechanical approach to working with the list. There is no need to follow the guidance she offers. I just find grace and Kaufman's approach (2016) helpful in bridging a Western sense of doing with effortless and spontaneous action. I believe at her core, Kaufman is writing about a way of being that is close to wu-wei and tzu-ran. "Grace allows us to walk lightly and easily, to treat others sweetly and gently, to receive and savor the gentleness of others. Grace in all its dimensions exists so we can move well through life" (270). Her words echo Slingerland's (2014) citation of Chuang Tsu's text "about individual wu-wei, about how you, as a person, can learn to move through the world in a free and easy way" (158–9).

Qi

In his book, Chuang-Tzu describes how qi *is* also helpful in nurturing wu-wei. A quote by Confucius says, "Do not listen with your ears but with your mind. Do not listen with your mind but with your vital energy. Ears can only hear, mind can only think, but vital energy is empty, receptive to all things. Tao abides in emptiness. Emptiness is the fasting of the mind" (Chuang Tsu 1974, 68). This vital energy is qi. Qi is what Ding referred to above when he said he was guided by "spiritual desires." Qi is a manifestation of the Way and Heaven and animates all things. Slingerland (2014) writes that "the spirit and the *qi* seem to be more or less synonymous: both provide one with a pipeline to Heavenly guidance" (145). We access qi by shutting down the conscious mind. Slingerland notes that this is much easier for children than adults and leads to their creativity. In adults, "incubation" can help in the process of quieting the thoughts and giving access to the unconscious and embodied knowing. This involves not focusing on the immediate problem but doing something else so the "unconscious mind is free to get on with its work" (147).

Chuang Tsu (1974) said, "The mind of a perfect mind is like a mirror. It grasps nothing. It expects nothing. If reflects but does not hold. Therefore the perfect man can act without effort" (159). Slingerland (2014) writes that Chuang Tsu's wu-wei is a "state of perfect equanimity, flexibility, and responsiveness" (158). This state is also described as "human on the outside, Heavenly on the inside" (182).

Contemplation and meditation, described in chapter 2, are a means to emptying and accessing qi. One of my students who had been doing meditation had an experience of being Heavenly on the inside when she wrote, "To my surprise feeling grew into *being* from the inside, which precipitated a sense of connectivity with the world. It was as though … I was lit up from the inside out" (Miller 2014, 157).

Another student wrote how her meditation led to an inner strength in her chest that can be seen as form of qi:

I have also been more able to extend this sense of compassion to myself when I have made a mistake or are in a moment of turmoil. In a very real sense, this meditative practice has helped me to feel as though there is a kind of strength in my chest, almost as though there is a rod running over my sternum. I am able to access this place of strength when I am challenged, but this strength is also gentle and forgiving. When I aggravated an injury this month, I was obviously frustrated and disappointed, fearing that I wouldn't be ready in time for an upcoming race. But the strength brought forward from this meditation helped me to see these feelings almost from a distance. I was able to understand why I was feeling those feelings, but the negative feelings weren't all consuming as they once were. There was this sense of internal strength, and forgiveness that I was able to extend to myself. (Anonymous Student Journal, 2021)

Loch Kelly (2019) has written a book about *effortless mindfulness*. He makes the contrast with Jon Kabat-Zinn's (2005) definition that reads: "Mindfulness means paying attention in a particular way; on purpose, in the present moment, and nonjudgmentally" (Kelly 2019, 4). "Effortless mindfulness is letting go of thoughts, present moments and attention-opening to naturally compassionate, nonconceptual awake awareness that is interconnected here and Now" (31). At the beginning of the book, Kelly (2019) connects this form of mindfulness to wu-wei since it does not involve a focused practice. He goes on to elaborate how effortless mindfulness is different from deliberate mindfulness. For example, instead of paying attention there is a letting go of attention so there can be what he calls "awake awareness" (32). Effortless mindfulness does not involve paying attention "on purpose" (32); instead, there is relaxation into awake awareness which can arise without our effort. The person also opens into a spacious awareness rather than focusing on one thing such as the breath. Also there is no effort to be "nonjudgmental" (32), but rather letting an innate, natural compassion arise. Effortless aware-ness also is rooted in interconnectedness so that the person is aware of the "body, emotions and thoughts from within and all around" (32).

Kelly's (2019) book is filled with ways to attain effortless mindfulness. He suggests just starting with awareness of the breath and body. How-ever, instead of keeping the focus on the breath, "feel the awareness that is aware." He also says to "allow your mind and thoughts to be as they are" and, as much possible, "feel the awareness that is aware." This awareness is alert, clear, and open and lies behind our thoughts and sensations. It accepts what is happening without trying to change anything. Gradually, we can have more moments of effortless mindfulness.

Effortless mindfulness is characterized by the following:

- The mind is wide open without an agenda.
- The thoughts are less prominent.
- Everything seems to be flowing freely and easily, happening naturally without any effort.
- There is a sense of joy and well-being not connected to what is happening.
- There is an awareness from boundless, interconnected, loving presence, rather than from a detached point of view. (Kelly 2019, 10)

Diana Winston (2019) has written a book about natural awareness, which is similar to effortless mindfulness. She describes the characteris-tics of natural awareness, which are very similar to effortless mindfulness. Here are a few of them:

- Your mind is like a wide-open space.
- You feel a sense of contentment not connected to external conditions.

- Everything seems to be happening on its own.
- You are simply being – without an agenda – and this beingness creates a feeling of timelessness and ease. (13)

Winston (2019) describes three forms of awareness. The first is focused awareness, which involves concentration on one object such as the breath. The second is flexible awareness, which includes concentration but also involves awareness of other objects such as feelings and thoughts. The third is natural awareness, which can arise spontaneously and involves a sense of well-being not dependent on surrounding conditions as well as awareness of all this is happening inside and outside us.

Here are two exercises from Winston's (2019) book:

ASK YOURSELF

Here's a question to ask yourself to help you access natural awareness. It is not meant for you to analyse and ruminate on but, rather, for you to simply drop into your receptive mind.

So get centered, relax, and try some breath awareness to calm your mind in meditation. Or in daily life, take a breath or two and then drop the following question in our mind, as if dropping a stone into a pond to notice the ripples. Listen deeply and see what emerges.

What is here now if there is no problem to solve? (61)

A MIRROR ANALOGY

After settling your mind a bit, read this analogy slowly and let the image sink in – not to dwell on it, but to see how it impacts your consciousness.

Imagine your mind is like a mirror, crystal clear, reflecting only what comes in front of it. No opinion, no clinging, no aversion – just pure reflection of reality exactly as it is. Rest your mind like a mirror that purely reflects what is right here in front of you. (96)

The work of Winston (2019) and Kelly (2019) can help teachers and students reach wu-wei in the classroom and in their lives.

De

De arises with wu-wei as one is empowered. People with de appeal to others because it is not contrived. There are various people with de described by Chuang Tsu (1974). Here is one:

> The true man of old slept without dreaming and woke without anxiety. His food was plain and his breath was deep. He stood straight and firm and did not waver. He was of humble mien but was not servile ... His radiance came from his inner light. He remained centered even in the company of others. (118)

It is difficult to describe de, but we can sense it intuitively. We are drawn to those who exhibit it as they are in tune with the Way, which usually helps people around them relax. Nothing seems forced. We can also feel "mellow and joyful" in their presence. De is similar to presence but differs because of its connection to the Way and Heaven, which includes a holistic and sacred quality.

Slingerland (2014) suggests that change occurs one person at a time when that person comes into contact with someone who has de. "Come into contact with them, and you are transformed, and then you go on to transform others" (160). However, it is possible if a teacher has de that he/she can reach several students. They can be moved in the way Makransky (2007) was awakened by the presence of his teacher, "Something was awakened in me by his presence, a deep desire to be like him and a recognition that somehow, mysteriously, I could. It made me grateful to be alive" (147).

Tom Culham (2013) writes about the relationship between Tao and de. "Thus *dao* despite being empty, formless, is present everywhere and is manifested in the world through its *de*, which transforms and nourishes the myriad things. *De* is an expression of *dao* in the world" (70). In the ancient Chinese document, *Techniques of the Mind Part 1*, there is this: "There is no gap between the Way and Inner power" (quoted in Culham 2013, 69). When we encounter de in another person we can become part of the Way. Their inner power helps us connect more deeply with the nature of things.

Returning to the chapter's main theme of wu-wei, Laurence Boldt (1999) writes:

In summary, we can say the ease comes from acting in harmony with the Tao in recognition of the unity of all things. Ease comes with respecting the way of nature and your own nature. Ease comes from honoring your intuition. Ease comes with a spirit of thanksgiving, of blessing and blessedness. Ease comes with moving from our innate strengths and gifts. Ease comes from doing what we are doing without using it as a means of trying to do or get something else. (103)

Chapter Five

Balancing Yin and Yang

Jing Lin (2006) describes these two qualities, "*yang* is the energy that creates and motivates and *yin* is the energy that nourishes, nurtures, sustains and harmonizes ... the balance of *yang* and *yin* preconditions the harmonious existence of nature and human beings" (80). This flow of energy between the two is essential to health of the cosmos, the Earth, society, and the human being. Eva Wong's (2015) translation of Chuang-Tzu describes how yin contains the seed of yang and how yang contains the seed of yin:

> Ultimate yin is cold and stern; ultimate yang is warm and bright. The sternness and coldness of ultimate yin comes from the heart of heaven's yang. The warmth and brightness of ultimate yang comes from the heart of earth's yin. These essences of yin and yang are embedded in their opposites so each already exists within the other. Yin and yang interact, copulate, comingle, and harmonize with each other bringing forth all life. (162)

This differs from the Western view that has independent polarities (e.g., good/bad, right/wrong, success/failure), which are difficult to reconcile. Anne Baring (2013) writes that Taoism is unique in its inclusion of the feminine: "Whereas the West imagined the creative ground of being as a transcendent Father, Taoism, more subtly and comprehensively than any other spiritual tradition nurtured the quintessence of the Feminine as a Primordial Mother, keeping alive the ancient feeling of relationship with Nature" (447). Baring's insight is important as the feminine connection to Nature is fundamental to healing the Earth.

Shunryu Suzuki (1973) has also written about yin and yang, "Good is not different from bad. Bad is good; good is bad. They are two sides of one coin" (103). In Wong's (2015) translation of Chuang-Tzu, she writes, "People today think that independence is a desirable thing, that yin and yang should be completely separated to each maintain its own identity … instead of embracing the interdependency of all things" (169). In contrast, the Sage is in harmony with yin and yang, "In stillness she is at one with the virtue of yin; in movement she flows with the action of yang" (153).

Ray Grigg (1994) describes how there is stillness at the centre of this movement of yin and yang: "In the *I Ching* it is represented as #52, Kan, when the *yang* of the mountain's thrust rests in momentary tranquility with the *yin* of the lake's downward waiting. It is that instant of seeming pause when all of the forces of the universe, as if waiting forever, are momentarily balanced in a massive stillness" (253).

One could argue that Western culture and education have been dominated by the yang, which tends to emphasize the rational, the material, the masculine, and the individual to the exclusion of the intuitive, the spiritual, the feminine, and the group. It could be said that this imbalance has led to sickness in the culture and institutions, including education.

Baring (2013) and others argue that the rise of the feminine is happening at a global level in an attempt to heal the Earth. For her, the word "feminine" stands for "the Soul and the unseen cosmic web of life that connects each one of us to all others and to the life of the planet and the greater life of the cosmos" (221). Baring also believes that the feminine principle is "rising to meet the masculine one in response to a deep soul impulse to balance and marry these archetypal energies within ourselves and within our world" (221). This awakening is closely linked to the environmental movement, respect for Indigenous perspectives which see the sacredness of nature, and the end of the oppression of women and their inclusion in creating a healthier world. It is interesting that it was a woman, Rachel Carson, and her 1962 book *Silent Spring*, that was instrumental in our awakening to the dangers of chemicals and pollutants. Through her work we began to radically change our view of nature and how we had to move away from exploiting the Earth and begin respecting its inherent beauty.

Recent research also suggests that educating women is important in addressing climate change:

As climate change and related issues have become the main challenge for the 21st century, educating girls is emerging as an important solution that has been largely overlooked and undervalued in the past. A recent study from Project Drawdown highlights educating girls as the #6 most impactful way to mitigate the impact of climate change, as it empowers girls to manage their reproductive health and increases their resilience and capacity. "They can be more effective stewards of food, soil, trees, and water, even as nature's cycles change." (Ricard, 2020)

The other event that was crucial in this transformation was seeing the Earth from space. Baring (2013) describes what so many people felt upon seeing this image: "In those few hours the sense of expansion was extraordinary, as our relationship with the cosmos and our perception of ourselves was transformed" (227). She also notes that it was significant that this took place from the moon, an age-old symbol of the feminine (yin). Astronauts and cosmonauts returning from space have elaborated on this new vision of the Earth and the cosmos. Here are Edgar Mitchell's (1996) words based on his 1971 Apollo 14 mission:

> What I experienced during that three-day trip home was nothing short of an overwhelming sense of the universal connectedness. I actually felt what has been described as an ecstasy of unity. It occurred to me that the molecules of my body and the molecules of the spacecraft itself were manufactured long ago in the furnace of one of the ancient stars that burned in the heavens about me ... the awe-inspiring beauty of the cosmos suddenly overcame me. While still aware of the separateness of my existence, my mind was flooded with an intuitive knowing that everything is interconnected-that this magnificent universe is a harmonious, directed, purposeful whole. And that we humans both as individuals and as a species, are an integral part of the ongoing process of creation. (3–4)

Baring (2013) suggests that, through the rise of the feminine, "we are beginning to recover the forgotten lunar consciousness of a feeling of relationship with a sacred Earth and a sacred Cosmos" (239).

Education

In the industrialized world education has leaned strongly towards the yang with its standardized testing and the accountability movement. The

Table 5.1. Balance between Yang and Yin in the Curriculum and the Classroom

Yang	Yin
Individual	Group
Content	Process
Knowledge	Imagination
Rational	Intuitive
Quantitative Assessment	Qualitative Assessment
Techniques/Strategies	Vision
Assessment/Evaluation	Instruction/Learning
Technology	Program
Whole	Part

Source: Miller (2019b, 10–12).

curriculum tends to focus on the development of skills with little attention to the development of the imagination and creativity. Using the Tao as a guide, we can try to develop a balance between yin and yang in the curriculum and the classroom. Table 5.1 and the comments that follow can provide a working outline.

Individual/Group: Education in North America has tended to emphasize individual competition rather than group collaboration. Although this has changed somewhat with greater emphasis being placed on cooperative learning, the current focus on testing and individual achievement strongly reinforces the yang energy in schools. Students compete against each other on standardized tests in order to move through the system and compete for university placements.

Content/Process: Covering the required content has often been at the centre of the curriculum and teaching. Ministries and departments of education set what must be covered in each grade or course. As a result, teachers feel pressure to make sure the material is covered. This approach does not make sense in a time where knowledge keeps evolving and changing. It can be argued that learning how to learn is a more important skill than memorizing material that the teacher gives or is in the textbook. Content needs to be seen in relation to skills that help the student learn so they can work together in a holistic manner.

Knowledge/Imagination: Curriculum reformers such as Hirsch, Kett, and Trefil (1988) have argued that there is certain essential knowledge that children should learn and this should take priority in teaching. Another view is that knowledge is co-created as students construct their own meaning and ways of knowing. Imagination plays an important role in this process. Recent curriculum reforms, however, have tended to emphasize covering content and testing how well students have mastered the content. In teaching a language, there is knowledge that needs to be learned (e.g., vocabulary) but that can still be taught in imaginative ways to engage the student.

Rational/Intuitive: Our education system and the culture as a whole have emphasized rational and linear approaches to problems. A more holistic approach calls for a merging of reason and intuition. When these two elements are connected, student thinking is enriched. However, approaches that emphasize intuition seem to rarely enter the classroom. The work of Iain McGilchrist (2009) has provided a broad perspective on the two sides of the brain and how they have influenced Western culture. He believes the West has been dominated by the left side of the brain:

> The left hemisphere is always engaged in a *purpose*; it always has an end in view, and downgrades whatever has not instrumental purpose in sight … The world of the left hemisphere, dependent on denotative language and abstraction, yields clarity and power to manipulate things that are known fixed, static, isolated, decontextualized, explicit, disembodied, general in nature, but ultimately lifeless. (174, emphasis in original)

In contrast, he believes that the right hemisphere

> … has no designs on anything. It is vigilant for whatever *is*, without preconceptions, without a predefined purpose … It yields a world of individual, changing, evolving, interconnected, implicit, incarnate, living beings within the context of the lived world, but in the nature of things never fully graspable, always imperfectly known – and to this world it exists in a relationship of care. (174, emphasis in original)

McGilchrist (2009) does not take a reductive approach to the brain. He does not see it as a machine but as part of nature that is open to what is and ultimately cannot be completely known. He argues that seeing the world from the left side of the brain contributes to fragmentation with the world "appearing to its inhabitants as if a collection of bits and pieces apparently randomly thrown together" (431). He also states that "over history intuition has lost ground to rationality" (437). Taoist/holistic education seeks to restore that lost ground and the balance between rationality and intuition.

Quantitative/Qualitative Assessment: Quantitative assessment is represented by the standardized test that tends to dominate in the age of accountability. Qualitative assessment is seen in the use of portfolios where a continuum of student work can be seen and assessed. Portfolios and other forms of qualitative assessment have made in-roads but students and teachers in elementary schools in the US have focused on the quantitative testing associated with the 2001 No Child Left Behind Act (Abeles 2015). It is important that qualitative methods are used to provide a broader picture of the student's development, particularly in the affective domain. An organic approach to accountability allows for more balance between the quantitative and qualitative.

Technique/Vision: In the West, we have tended to focus on technique. In education, this has meant an excessive emphasis on teaching and assessment strategies without a corresponding link to a broader conception of learning and a vision of the whole child. In contrast, educators such as Maria Montessori and Rudolf Steiner offer a balance between technique and a vision of the whole person. Teaching strategies and evaluation methods are developed in relation to this vision of the whole person. An example of this is Montessori's cosmic education, which was mentioned in the first chapter.

Assessment/Learning: Education in the twenty-first century has stressed testing and reporting mostly in the form of standardized testing. When this emphasis becomes so strong, we lose our focus on learning, particularly natural, organic learning processes. Curriculum becomes teaching to the test rather than the facilitation of learning. A balance needs to be restored between assessment and learning. Anna Quindlen (2005) who was a commentator for *Newsweek* wrote: "Our education system is broken; accountability and standards will fix it. This is the mantra of government testing programs, from local certifications to the federal No Child Left Behind program, which might as well be called No Child Left Untested."

Countries such as Singapore, which at one time put a strong emphasis on standardized testing, are moving away from that approach. Finland, whose international scores are high, has no standardized testing.

Technology/Program: Another current obsession is technology. Some educators argue that we need a computer or an iPad for every child in the classroom. Again, a broader programmatic vision is needed to set technology in a proper context. A technology driven curriculum is ultimately a narrow and limited curriculum. The use of technology needs to be placed in the larger context of the program's overall vision. Technology and the internet do have the capacity to let students make a variety of connections and these should be pursued.

Whole/Part: There is also the relation between the whole and the part, as holistic teaching seeks to keep the two in balance. Generally, we have focused on the part as we have broken the curriculum into subjects, units, and lessons, yet we lack an encompassing vision that inspires us. In the holistic curriculum we attempt to link the unit and lesson to a larger vision of the whole child, nature, and Earth.

The Wallas Model

Graham Wallas (1926) described a model of creative thinking that uses both right and left brain thinking and thus a balance of yin and yang. The first stage is *preparation* where the individual gathers information relevant to the problem or project and is more yang. The second step, which is more yin, involves *incubation*, as the individual relaxes and does not make an effort to work consciously on the problem. Instead, it is suggested that the images realign themselves in the individual as he/she consciously attends to something else. In the third stage of *illumination* (yin), the solution can arise, often spontaneously through the appearance of an insight or image. The fourth stage is *verification*, or *revision*, which is more yang and is where the individual puts the idea into use and consciously works with the idea in a more detailed manner.

Alan Watts (1999) also has written about incubation as part of problem solving:

> Now, if you want to find an intelligent solution to a problem, your brain can do the work ... However, most people never use their brains; they use their minds instead and they use their minds the same way they use their muscles. You can strain your head just as if it were a muscle, and work very hard trying to arrive at an answer, but it doesn't really work that way. When you really want to find an answer to something, what you need to do is contemplate the problem. Visualize your question as well as you can, and then simply wait. If you don't and if instead you try to find the solution through brute mental strength, you may be disappointed, because any solution that comes in that way is likely to be wrong. But when you have waited for a while, the solution will come of itself. (12)

The Wallas model, and other models of creative thinking, are useful educators in balancing analysis and insight in classroom pedagogy. Visualization, meditation, and various aesthetic experiences can be used to enhance incubation and illumination, while logical problem-solving models can be used to facilitate preparation and verification. Effective thinking, then, involves both intuition and analysis.

Here is an expanded version of the Wallas model that employs both right and left brain thinking. I have made some modifications to the Wallas approach to include the following steps:

- Uncertainty/Ambiguity
- Problem Clarification
- Preparation/Frameworking
- Incubation
- Alternative Search
- Illumination/Alternative Selection
- Verification

Uncertainty/Ambiguity: Most problem solving is prodded by an unresolved situation. For example, in writing this book, the lack of clarity about Taoist approaches to teaching and learning was a factor that encouraged me to explore this area in more depth. I needed to examine the relationship between Taoism and holism and the implications for teaching and learning. In my course, The Holistic Curriculum, I make reference to the Tao; and, in teaching the course in the summer of 2019, four Chinese students made a presentation on Taoism. Two of these students, Tian and Xiang, wrote papers that impressed me and we met after the course about the possibility of writing a book together.

Problem Clarification: In this step, the person or group attempts to get some sort of handle on the problem. This might be done by writing out a problem statement. Unlike logical, mathematical problem solving, the problem statement is not a hypothesis in the technical sense; instead, it attempts to get at the root of the problem. Imagery and intuition can be used at this stage to help sort out the problem; by inner reflection the central issue may come forth. The problem statement for this book is, How can Taoism facilitate teaching and learning and what is the relationship of a Taoist approach to teaching to holistic education?

Preparation/Frameworking: Here one attempts to develop a more complete framework for the problem in order to see the problem from a broader perspective. For this book, this involved developing an outline in the form of chapter headings. This step tends to involve more linear thinking as each aspect of the framework is explored; however, imagery and intuition can still be at play here. It is possible, for example, for one to have an image of either part of the framework or a vision of the entire approach. The image of yin and yang of course is central to Taoism and is one of the key images for this book.

Incubation: Incubation can occur throughout the problem-solving process. In fact, although these steps are presented in a linear order, the approach I am describing is really much more fluid and is not a step-by-step process. Incubation involves a standing back and letting the elements work themselves through at a subconscious level. If we force the problem-solving process too much, then it will be much less productive. In working on this book, as well as on others I have written, I often found ideas popping into my head while meditating, walking, driving, or taking a bath.

Alternative Search: This usually involves a more conscious search for alternatives as well as an examination of the alternatives. Alternative courses of action are first explored and developed, and then judged against criteria. These criteria can be developed consciously and can include a number of factors, or only a few which are felt more intuitively. Ultimately, these criteria are usually related to the framework. It is also possible that examining alternatives can change the original framework. Again, this whole problem-solving process tends to go back and forth rather than being a logical sequence. Working with Tian and Xiang allowed me to get feedback on concepts such as yin and yang and wu-wei.

Illumination/Alternative Selection: Here the person settles on a course of action. This can involve a rational assessment of the alternatives against the criteria or it may involve the appearance of an image. If an image or intuitive insight does occur, it can also be assessed against the criteria; but we have to be careful that our criteria and mindset don't become too rigid. If the criteria are too inflexible, creativity will be stifled. If the vision is a powerful one, the criteria themselves may have to be reworked. Here, the outline for this book was the course of action so that we could move forward together in the writing of the book.

Verification: Now the solution must be tested. In short, does it work, or must you search for other solutions? When the manuscript was completed for this book, we sent it for review. We knew the reviewers could recommend alternatives, which could range from reworking small sections of the text to reorganizing and rewriting a large amount of material. The reviewers were an important first step in the verification of this book, and a second step in the verification would come from the type of readership the book would develop.

This model can also be applied to problems and projects that students confront in different subjects. For example, the problem of whether a nation should be part of a larger trading bloc was very relevant as I was writing this book: the United States, Canada, and Mexico had just completed renegotiating the North American Free Trade Agreement (NAFTA). So the model could be applied as follows.

Uncertainty/Ambiguity: Here, the uncertainty focuses on what issues are at stake in joining a trading bloc. Issues usually focus on loss of national control (e.g., tariffs) on some industries versus possible economic gains. However, issues are not just limited to economics, as culture is often affected. Thus, students could examine possible effects on the arts as well as the economic implications.

Problem Clarification: Should my country be part of a large trading bloc (e.g., NAFTA)?

Preparation/Frameworking: In this step, students attempt to see the underlying issues that affect the decision to be part of a large trading bloc. Some people see a conflict between two groups: business interests and environmental groups. Business and large corporations argue that free trade will enhance the economy and create more jobs. From another perspective, there is concern that large trading blocs override local interests, which include environmental concerns. Science, then, can be included in this unit to examine relevant environmental issues.

Incubation: Let the students step back from the problem for a while. They can discuss the issues involved; but it can be helpful just to let things sit (e.g., a few days) as they grapple with the issues and their vision of what interests are most important.

Alternative Search: Here the students deal with the issue more consciously as they develop their vision more clearly and examine what the consequences are of each position. The students approach this systematically by writing out their position and listing the advantages and disadvantages of having joined a free trade bloc. Their vision becomes the criteria for assessing being part of NAFTA.

Illumination/Alternative Selection: The students decide whether they believe being part of a trading bloc is positive or negative. After the more systematic alternative search, the students can step back again and do some more reflection on the decision. After the inner reflection, there is a greater chance that the decision will not be an abstract one but one more connected to the whole person. The student can then write down their decision and the reasons for it.

Verification: In this last step, the students can share their answers with other students and the teacher. They can also compare it to other student responses.

Fred Rogers

In chapter 3, I discuss the work of Fred Rogers as an example of including the feminine in education. Rogers was truly a holistic educator who combined yin and yang in his television program *Mr. Rogers' Neighborhood*. Rogers saw himself as an educator, not an entertainer. In one talk Rogers said, "One of the major goals of education must be to help students dis-cover a greater awareness of their unique selves, in order to increase their feelings of personal worth, responsibility and freedom" (quoted in King, 2018, 328). Ellen Galinksy (2007), president of the Families and Work Institute, commented, "He [Fred] connects on an intellectual and a social and emotional level all at once. He cares about people." Rogers believed that feelings were very important and should always be considered along with the other information that was shared. His shows dealt with difficult topics like divorce and death and how it was important to talk about chil-dren's feelings when these events happened.

There was a contemplative quality to his program because it was slow paced. Rogers included periods of space and silence. In Rogers's biogra-phy, Maxwell King (2018), his biographer, writes, "Silence – Fred's willing-ness, as a producer and as person, to embrace quiet, inactivity and empty space – and his calm demeanor were completely unexpected in television in the 1970s. These were qualities that captivated children and their parents" (194). We can see Taoist virtues here such as silence, emptiness, and calm-ness. Rogers was also concerned about nurturing the inner life of the child.

People commented that Rogers himself had a "feminine quality of mother love," yet he also had a strong intellect and a "steely core" (quoted in King 2018, 119, 202). Rogers embodied yin and yang in himself.

Embodying Yin and Yang

Yin and yang exist within us and it is important to allow both to flow freely. For centuries in the West, men were expected to express yang energy by being strong, tough, and not expressing feelings. Women were expected to express yin energy through being caring, expressing their feelings, and avoiding intellectual pursuits. Today, we are moving away from those ste-reotypes and towards an acceptance that allows people from both sexes to embrace both yin and yang.

Contemplation and movement practices such as qigong, tai chi, yoga, and meditation allow yin and yang to flow freely within the human being and promote self-cultivation (discussed in chapter 3). Hua-Ching Ni (1997) writes, "By practicing self-cultivation techniques, one develops a sensitivity to the energies constantly circling within the body" (36). One of my students noted the flow of energy in his body during the meditation:

> Tingling and buzzing in the extremities was very common. I intuited that it is energy flowing through the body. If I stop typing right now, I feel it as well, although I am not normally aware of it. That tingling and buzzing also was prominent around my head, across my face, at the top of my head and focused in between the eyebrows. I know some of those spaces are home to chakras. There are also things about synchronization between the hemispheres occurring during sitting practice. All of these sensations were extremely subtle for the most part, however, on a few occasions they were intense and it was hard to focus on the counting. Mostly when these experiences arose, I accepted them and tried to focus on the counting, treating them as nothing special. (Anonymous Student Journal, 2021)

Awareness of energy in the body allows it to flow more freely as well as the nurturing the relationship between yin and yang.

Ni (1997) goes on to say,

> By utilizing in our lives the same cosmic principles which assure the harmonious functioning of the universe itself, we can nurture our vital energy and establish the internal balance necessary for a happy life. The principles treasured by ancient and modern Sages are simplicity, equilibrium, harmony, and quietude. These principles display the practical value of allowing one's energy to evolve and function normally. By personifying these cosmic principles, we come to realize that we embody the entire universe. Microcosm and macrocosm become one. (37)

One of my students, after completing her meditation practice, described how doing loving-kindness meditation brought a positive energy to her classroom:

> Given my positive experiences with meditation, I believe contemplative practices are vital to a healthy classroom environment, benefitting both teachers and students. Similar to our class now, I would begin each day with a *metta* meditation (provided this was okay with parents) as I believe it opens our hearts and cultivates love, compassion, and a safe environment. Even if not resembling a

traditional meditation practice, for at least 15 minutes daily I believe students should have the opportunity to just be. This is something I wish had been incorporated in my classes as a student. (Anonymous Student Journal, 2021)

Yin and yang flow at every level – the cosmos, Earth, cultures, institutions, classrooms, and the individual, and being aware of them can help cultivate the harmonious well-being of ourselves, our institutions, and our cultures.

Qi

Tom Culham and Jin Lin (2020) write about qi and its relationship to virtue:

> Laozi [Lao-Tzu] posits that virtues such as kindness compassion humility and selfless giving help one reach a state of tranquility and enhance one's qi. He held the universe functions in this way as well as human society and individuals. Thus qi, values and virtue are intimately related. The outcome of the process of working towards alignment with virtue is an enhancement of one's own life energy, qi. The more one is in alignment with virtue, the more qi you will have and the more you will experience virtue. (74)

We can develop qi by nurturing the virtues of humility and caring described in chapter 2 of this book. Qi can also be developed through various disciplines such as qigong, tai chi, yoga, and various forms of contemplation.

The classroom is also an energy system. The concepts of yin and yang can help maintain interest and energy in the classroom. If either yin or yang dominates, qi will dissipate, so the two need to be seen as complementary and in relationship. However, it is not about maintaining a 50/50 balance but allowing both to manifest. The teacher needs to use his/her intuition to know when to bring more yin or more yang into the classroom. For example, if there has been too much teacher-directed learning (yang), the teacher can use small groups (yin) to reenergize that classroom. Similarly, if there has been an excessive focus on right-brain activities such as intuitive thinking, there could be a shift to more rational and logical thinking.

Chapter Six

Taoism and Holistic Education

Holistic education emerged as a term in the 1980s and has continued to grow and expand as a field. However, its roots go back to Indigenous Peoples and their approach to education as described by Indigenous scholars such Four Arrows (2012) and Greg Cajete (1994). It also includes the great teachers of the Axial Age (Buddha, Confucius, Socrates, Ezekiel), the work of Rousseau and Pestalozzi, the Transcendentalists, Montessori education, and Waldorf education. The common thread is the focus on reaching the whole child – body, mind, and spirit. Mahatma Gandhi (1980) was also a holistic educator who communicated with Maria Montessori and wrote this:

> I hold that true education of the intellect can only come through a proper exercise and training of the bodily organs, e.g., hands, feet, eyes, ears, nose, etc. In other words an intelligent use of the bodily organs in a child provides the best and quickest way of developing his intellect. But unless the development of the mind and body goes hand in hand with a corresponding awakening of the soul, the former alone would prove to be a poor lopsided affair. By spiritual training I mean education of the heart. A proper and all round development of the mind, therefore, can take place only when it proceeds with the education of the physical and spiritual faculties of the child. They constitute an indivisible whole. According to this theory, therefore, it would be a gross fallacy to suppose that they can be developed piecemeal or independently of one another. (138)

I believe that most departments and ministries of education have committed the "gross fallacy" that Gandhi refers to. The focus is on the head with some reference to the body while completely ignoring the heart and the soul.

Whole Teaching

To reach the head, hands, and heart of the student, we need a broad range of teaching approaches that reach the whole child. A central theme is an inclusive approach to teaching that attempts to approach the child as an "indivisible whole." Specifically, it focuses on how teachers can use and integrate three basic approaches: transmission, transaction, and transformation. Using these approaches in an integrative way is what I call "whole teaching." Let's look briefly at the approaches.

Transmission teaching involves the student receiving and accumulating knowledge and skills – for example, by reading a textbook or listening to a teacher's explanation. Transmission teaching is appropriate when we begin to learn a particular skill. For example, when we learn to drive a car, we study the basic rules of driving by reading the driving handbook in preparation for a written test.

Transactional teaching involves the student in solving a problem or pursuing some form of inquiry – usually based on a set of procedures, which may be rooted in a particular discipline, such as physics or history. There is a focus on thinking skills.

Transformational teaching connects the student and the curriculum more deeply – for example, through such strategies as cooperative learning, drama, and role playing. Transformational teaching nourishes the student's inner life (Miller and Seller 1985; Miller 2010).

Using the three positions, teachers can develop a rhythm in their teaching. Individual teachers can find their own rhythm that fits their subject and their own inclinations; using the three approaches in a rhythmic manner helps create energy in the classroom. If the teacher just stays with one approach, inevitably the energy will diminish. Maintaining and creating energy is central to Taoism, and in the previous chapters I wrote briefly about qi. Using the three positions in a rhythmic manner can help foster qi in the classroom. For example, I start my classes with loving-kindness meditation (transformation). Then I give a short lecture (transmission) followed by a small group discussion where students discuss the ideas presented in the lecture (transaction). In every class, I try to employ each of the three positions.

Holistic education attempts to be in harmony with the basic nature of things, which includes interconnectedness and interdependence at all levels of the universe. In Taoism, everything is seen as part of the whole, the Tao. Chuang-Tzu said, "Great knowledge sees all in one. Small knowledge breaks down in to the many" (quoted in Boldt 1999, xxviii). Unfortunately, education in most countries is "small knowledge," where everything is broken down into separate subjects, units, and lessons with bits of information. There is a focus on individual achievement as students compete against one another. Holistic education seeks an education that lets students see they are in relationship with each other, the Earth, and the cosmos.

Taoism also suggests that if we live our lives in harmony with nature and the way of things, health and well-being will arise. All beings will prosper both physically and spiritually. As mentioned in the second chapter, holistic education should also foster the student's well-being and compassion for others. The main aims of holistic education include the development of *wisdom, compassion, and well-being.* Wisdom involves seeing deeply into the nature of things and acting accordingly with that awareness. It involves seeing ourselves in relationship and not as isolated egos; this sense of connection can give rise to compassion because we see ourselves connected to all forms of life. Holistic education also nurtures well-being. Happiness can also arise. Over the past couple of decades, there has been increasing interest and research in happiness. One country, Bhutan, has as its main goal the achievement of "gross national happiness." People who are happy and experience well-being tend to contribute more to society than those who are angry and unhappy.

Curriculum of Connections

To be in harmony with the Way, holistic education focuses on connectedness. I have identified six connections in my book *The Holistic Curriculum* (2019a) – Earth connections, subject connections, community connections, thinking connections, body-mind connections, and soul connections. This book helped the Equinox Holistic Alternative School in Toronto develop its curriculum using the six connections as a framework. Founded in 2009, Equinox is the largest alternative school in the Toronto District School Board and has a long waiting list of families who would like to enroll their children (https://equinoxschool.ca). Equinox is a K–8 school with two hundred students. It is housed in a building that contains another school, Roden Public School, and is located in the east end of Toronto in a neighbourhood known as Little India. It sits on a large lot covered with trees and grass.

I have had the privilege of being connected with the school since a group of teachers and parents began developing the proposal for the school in 2007. In 2015, I conducted a qualitative study of the school where I interviewed nine teachers and the principal, and nine parents and nine students, including four former students who were by then in high school (Miller 2016). The study along with other data show that the holistic curriculum can support public schools in developing programs that not only educate the whole child but help the child flourish. In April of 2018, I attended an event at the school where teachers and parents discussed the school's vision. Again, I was impressed by the positive energy and strong sense of community that the school has been able to maintain since its inception. A principal from a prestigious private school visited Equinox and said "this school has soul." There has been interest from people in different countries, including Spain, Korea, and Norway. In October 2017, I gave a talk on whole child education and Equinox in Oslo (Miller 2017).

The mission of the school as stated in its Staff Handbook reads: "To engage hearts, bodies, minds and spirits of students in a learning environment that instils a love, respect and understanding of what is around them, igniting their natural curiosity through mentorship, so they may choose to honour and value the world around them" (Equinox Holistic Alternative School [EHAS] 2017/2018, 2). In my study of the school, teachers, parents, and students clearly support this mission. Both teachers and parents believe the vision is about reaching the "head, hands and heart" of the students. One parent said this about the vision, "It means encouraging kids to think in all different directions. Integrated subject matter. Also thinking about themselves and their communities. Self- knowledge, coming into your own as a person." She added that "it worked well for her daughter." One student who attended Equinox and was in high school said that school "focuses on the whole child. Not just teaching academics." She added, "Really teaches the entire body" (Miller 2016). As noted above, I interviewed four former students who attended Equinox and were by then in high school and I was impressed by how thoughtful and articulate they were.

I also asked whether the school was meeting the expectation of teaching the whole child. Everyone I interviewed felt that it was. One parent whose daughter was in high school said, "It surpassed my expectations because I see how well adjusted she is." Her daughter was on the honour role in high school. Another mother whose son was bullied in another school said, "Equinox met my expectations. It was amazing, wonderful. I had peace of mind sending him there." Another commented on how she witnessed compassion and empathy in the children at Equinox. A parent agreed with this and said that her boys "care more about others and they care more about the planet." Several parents commented on the quality of the teachers there. Finally, one parent said this:

> It was an *incubator* where they could mature at their own rate. So much emphasis on conflict resolution, experiencing the difference of others, and accepting others. Kids could grow up without experiencing the pressures in other schools that I hear about. Gaining the core sense of self is so important as you are gaining independence and going out into the world. Going into high school and not needing to be "cool." All of her friends from Equinox are really different from each other but they all connect with each other and accept each other as being different. It is lovely. (Miller 2016, 298)

The concept of *incubator* can be seen as a Taoist approach, as students are allowed to grow and develop without too much interference from the teachers. Another way of putting this is that teachers practise their own form of wu-wei in working with students by allowing students to develop in their own way. The high school students I interviewed agreed with this statement. One girl said that it helped her develop self-confidence, while one boy said that at Equinox he learned it was "OK to be different." He added that he could build "his own platform as an individual. Equinox helps you do that." The teachers generally agreed that the school was meeting expectations. One teacher who had been there for several years described it as a "journey" and that the school was clearly developing in a "positive direction." Another teacher said the school is "a harbour for parents and teachers who care about sustainable living." One teacher commented about" the authenticity you see in the kids." She added that "students are honored for who they are" (Miller 2016).

The experience at Equinox will help describe the six connections.

Earth connections. Taoism is based on seeing nature and acting in accordance with its ways. Nature is seen as a guide for how to live and thus be in harmony with the Earth and its processes. Equinox has made the Earth connection one of its main priorities. The Staff Handbook has this statement about this connection:

> Equinox believes in the importance of children both understanding and connecting to the Earth. Exploring nature allows children to have awe-inspiring moments through realizing larger-than-life natural processes and happenings, instils feelings of calm, reduces stress, allows for physical activity, and promotes risk-taking. The interconnectedness of the natural world is emphasized. Older students begin to learn about environmental issues and work towards becoming stewards of the land.
>
> The outdoor education program is a cornerstone of Equinox's holistic curriculum. The most effective way to teach about the earth, environmental phenomena and processes and features of the natural world is to actually be teaching and learning in the outdoor classroom. The kindergarten program is largely outdoors with weekly local nature hikes. Students in Grades 1–8 spend time outside each day. Through repeated hands-on experiences with a wide range of fields, students develop resiliency and the skills needed to safely reconnect with nature. From Kindergarten on, we are outside year round, in all weather, requiring children to make good choices and experience the results. Students are given ample opportunities to stretch out of their comfort zones. By facing challenges out of doors, students discover more of their inner resources of adaptability, problem-solving cooperation, curiosity, gratitude and vitality. (EHAS 2017/2018, 4–5)

The day at Equinox begins with students from each class first meeting outside in circles to do exercises, meditation, and some sharing. As mentioned in the Staff Handbook, the kindergarten students spend most of the day outside. Fortunately, there are many areas close to the school that allow for being in nature. These include Ashbridges Estates, a ravine, and other parks. Another place that students have visited is the Brickworks where, one year, they did a pond study during the early days of spring. Parents again were involved and set up learning stations there. One station focused on plants, another on birds, and one on insects. At the end they had a scavenger hunt that involved a mapping exercise that consolidated the whole experience. One parent commented that her child's experience of the pond study in a previous school was going to the pond and filling out a worksheet. She said, "It was different from the pond study at Equinox where they were really engaged."

In all the outdoor experiences the students keep a *nature journal*. Students learn observation skills and to record their observations. There is also a lot of freedom to inquire, draw, and measure. Sometimes the students even write songs based on their observations. These journals become books that the students keep over several grades. One teacher said, "Their books have to feel authentic to me. So, everything has to mean something. Our principal showed the books to other principals."

One parent commented how being outside allowed for positive interactions between students:

> I saw one boy who was known as bully in his previous school working with a girl. She was an artistic, creative person who had been bullied in her previous school. She was teaching him about knot tying and I saw all those barriers and labels falling away. How would they have interacted in typical classroom setting? It is outside and they feel less exposed. I also saw kids working cooperatively on projects together. It seemed to happen so organically. It was amazing. (Miller 2016, 296)

"Happening organically" allows nature to work its magic on how the students relate to one another and is in the spirit of a Taoist approach to learning.

Fan Yang, Jing Lin, and Thomas Culham (2019) in their article about Taoist philosophy call for a love-based approach to environmental education (EE): "From intimidation to love, love-based EE is a process of enhancing public environmental awareness through reasoning and empathy, which will enable people to love, respect, and be grateful to nature, thereby to take active actions to solve present and future environmental problems and construct an eco-friendly world" (1127). Equinox's approach to Earth education is also a love-based approach.

Subject connections. Taoism, as articulated earlier in this chapter by Chuang-Tzu, focuses on "great knowledge" that sees how everything is connected and is part of the whole. Holistic education seeks to show relationships between the subjects and to integrate subjects into theme-based learning. Here is the statement about subject connections from the school's Staff Handbook:

> Equinox uses a cross-curricular approach to integrate subjects. Subjects are woven together around broad themes. This creates richer learning opportunities and strong cognitive links. For instance, the arts – drama, visual arts, music and dance – are integrated into all of the language arts programs wherever possible so that children learn the curricular material in fun and creative ways. Learning with head, heart and mind, children educated through this holistic education approach deeply understand, retain and recall the content. (EHAS 2017/2018, 5)

One example of how Equinox integrates subjects was a year-long study of salmon. There was a salmon hatchery in a junior classroom. Students could see the growth of salmon. Math and science inquiry activities were developed around the salmon. One parent commented that this project brought all the subjects together. She said, "They were learning different subjects without realizing that they were learning. It was magical. I have seen the development of critical thinking, inquiry, and love of learning." They created a large mural around the salmon. Another parent commented, "They did art around salmon and they learned so much about salmon. It was so integrated – they wrote, they thought, they measured. What a beautiful, holistic thing. This was an incredible year and the kids did the salmon dance at the end of the year." In the spring, the salmon were released into the river and students from both Equinox and Roden participated. There is a film documentary of the salmon run. Part of the experience also included a silent, meditative walk. The teacher commented that, in their written reflections on the whole project, students wrote about the power of the silent walk. The salmon project is also an example of using nature as a way to integrate learning.

Community connections. Yang, Lin, and Culham (2019) write about how we should see all other life as siblings. "Taoists view all kinds of species on earth as siblings, based on the basic Taoist belief that ten thousand beings (meaning all beings) were all generated from Tao. Taoism persuades people to care about wildlife with compassion, respecting them as human beings' siblings or relatives, even if they are tiny insects or invisible living things" (1124).

The holistic curriculum should foster what Martin Luther King Jr. called the beloved community at all levels. The most immediate community is the classroom, and cooperative education with its emphasis on learning teams attempts to foster community within the classrooms. Ideally, the school as a whole should be a community, or a sanctuary, in Lance Secretan's (1996) terms. It is also important for the school to extend itself into the surrounding community and there are programs that involve the student in community service or social change activities. Finally, global education attempts to connect the student to the global community.

When I interviewed the teachers, students, and parents, they frequently talked about the love they felt in the Equinox community. Here is the statement about community in the school's Staff Handbook: "Equinox has put a great effort into building a cohesive school community. From the small staff and open-concept educational space, to the eager parents and volunteers that play an integral role in the day-to-day functioning of the school, Equinox prides itself on being a communal, close-knit and welcoming space" (EHAS 2017/2018, 6).

When I interviewed staff, parents, and students, there were several comments about the strength of the community. Here are the comments of two parents. One father said, "There is a special sense of community. When a father of one of the kids died, it brought the community even closer together." One mother talked about how being involved with the school had changed her life. "We look after each other helping with kids, picking them up at school, doing a dinner, etc. The school has given us a bigger picture of life. Rather than just working for survival, we are working for a better world." Community is developed through rituals, looping, and the use of circles. The school holds several rituals and ceremonies through the year to build community, some of which are described here.

Acorn Ceremony: One of the first ceremonies of the school year is the Acorn Ceremony when the Grade 8 students welcome the new kindergarten students and give each one an acorn. The new students walk under a rainbow bridge. There is a set of special chairs that is also included to help give a sense of continuity to the ceremony. It is held outside with lots of parents in attendance and one of the parents tells a story. This ceremony is also used to welcome new teachers to the school.

Day of the Dead: Students go home and interview their parents and then they write biographies of past family members. On the Day of the Dead, they bring pictures of some of these individuals. A table and altar are set up and there is Mexican music and food. One teacher commented, "It was so beautiful when we honoured the father of one of the staff here." After lunch the students go into their classes, sit in a circle, and read their biographies. One student brought in a song that connected her with her grandfather. A teacher commented, "They also can choose a public figure and one student picked Robin Williams who [had just died] and his description was very deep and beautiful." The students can also honour a pet that has died.

Earth Day: Another large event that includes the whole community and is held on the beach at Ashbridges Park. Students are broken into small groups – clans. Each clan does something special such as dressing up as an animal. The older students go first and build a labyrinth in the sand. One year the school focused on bees in the curriculum and many students worked together to build a giant bee sculpture. A lot of thought and planning goes into the event as there are activities and games all day. The day usually ends with singing.

Graduation: Students graduating from Grade 8 mark their graduation by taking a special trip together, which involves going outdoors for two days and staying in tents. One night involved being on your own for the whole night. One parent commented that after the trip the students were asked what they learned and they said that things do not always go the way you think they will, an important life lesson. One student who is now in high school said the experience was "amazing."

Three other practices include looping, circles, and restorative justice.

Looping is when students stay with one teacher for more than one year. The mother of one student who was in the classroom of the same teacher for several years commented, "The teacher was able to work with each student and draw on their strengths and really make them part of a community." A teacher who worked with students for more than one year could witness real growth in the students.

Circles are used in a variety of ways. Every morning the classes meet outside in circles where they do meditation, yoga, qigong, and other activities together. Circles have also been used to deal with behavioural issues. One teacher said: "I meet with students in a circle when there is a problem.

We also do this as teachers. People actually practise what they preach here. It is wonderful."

The school uses restorative justice to deal with behavioural issues. Here is the statement of restorative justice from the school's Staff Handbook:

> When facing interpersonal challenges in relationships, we rely on the wisdom and methods of Restorative Justice to develop a healthy school environment. In striving to operate as a community, with students taking ownership and responsibility for learning and relating, and teachers taking a power-with-students approach, the major rewards include skill building, creative fulfillment and personal growth. Through this process, we all learn to be accountable for our actions in meaningful, direct ways. (EHAS 2017/2018, 11)

Thinking connections. The holistic curriculum seeks a balance between logical, analytic thinking and intuitive, holistic thinking. In chapter 5, I referred to the work of Iain McGilchrist (2009) who has written about the two sides of the brain and how both need to be supported through various teaching strategies. In Taoism there is constant reference to the centre where both forms of thinking can work. "It means that we can scrutinize details and yet hold a vast view" (Wong 1997, 99). Yang, Lin, and Culham (2019) write about how emotions and reason need to be integrated: "Emotions and feelings need to be combined with reason, and integrated under the ethos of love and respect, and many methods can be found in implementing love-based EE" (1127). Strategies such as visualization, art, exploring metaphor, and writing poetry are ways to nurture intuition. At Equinox, the Staff Handbook refers to intuition and intellect connections:

> A major focus at Equinox is **inquiry-based** or **problem-based** approaches to learning. Inquiry-based approaches are primarily used in our science and outdoor education program. The educator poses open-ended questions that encourage the students to be curious and inquire about the answer on their own. With the educator posing and guiding intentional questions, this forms the basis of scientific inquiry, develops intuition and independent thinking, sparks curiosity and encourages deep thinking. In the outdoor education program, teachers (and some parents) are trained in an approach called *The Art of*

Questioning, to pose inquiry-based questions to their students in the outdoor classroom.

In math, students are given a problem to solve. There are many different ways to solve the math problem and the students are free to choose their own way of solving the problem. Students often work in cooperative groupings with this method, learning effectively how to communicate with others, listen and respect other points of view and negotiate a solution.

Both inquiry-based and problem-based approaches help to make the connection between intellect and intuition. With these methods, the students are encouraged to rely on their own knowing and ability to solve problems. This process of discovery helps students to take ownership of their learning and to trust their inner knowing. As students become familiar with this process, they get used to accessing their intuition to solve problems. Similarly, many of the mindfulness activities practiced in the school help to develop the intuition. (EHAS 2017/2018, 6, emphasis in original)

One example of this approach is the knowledge building circle. The teacher sits outside the circle and introduces a question. For example, should we go to the zoo? The students then raise other questions and take responsibility and control of the process while the teacher takes notes. In the primary grades, the inquiry centres on the elements such as water, air, and fire that young children wonder about. The children develop their own questions and write down the questions and answers in their own books. The students document the inquiry in these books.

One of the former students I interviewed who was by then in high school commented on the impact of the intuition/inquiry-based approach. "They found interesting ways to teach us … This really got the information into your brain and [it stays] there. Rather than forgetting it in two days. I liked the focus on the arts."

Body-mind connections. In the third chapter I referred to how embodiment is central to Taoism. As expressed in *Wen-tzu*, "So facial expressions can reach where talk cannot" (quoted in Cleary 2003c,179).

Richard Davidson and Sharon Begley (2012) have done extensive research on the mind-body relationship. They have found that there is a bidirectional relationship between the mind and body so "that the state of the mind influences the body, and the state of the body influences the mind" (136). They suggest that the body "can become an ally in transforming emotion, meaning practices that emphasize the body, such as hatha yoga, have the potential to modulate emotion" (136). They work in the fields of behavioural medicine and health psychology and write that "the emotional state itself predicts the health problems" (115).

In *How the Body Knows the Mind*, Susan Beilock (2015) summarizes much of the recent research on how the body influences the mind. She also writes about how the body impacts learning:

> Both moving your foot and understanding the word *kick* are governed, in part, by an area of the motor cortex that controls the leg. It's hard to separate the reading mind from the doing mind. Teaching words estranged from the objects and actions they refer to doesn't reflect how the brain is organized. Because our body and mind are tightly connected, the body is an important part of the learning process. (50)

Beilock (2015) describes a program called Math Dance, which is a series of whole-body mathematical activities. This program is "designed to give people the physical experience of an abstract idea" (57). She quotes Maria Montessori's comment that "mental development must be connected with movement and be dependent on it" (56). Beilock argues that schools today ignore the impact of the body on learning and gives many examples of how movement can be incorporated into the learning process.

Yang, Lin, and Culham (2019) write about the importance of embodied learning from a Taoist perspective. They say: "Embodied knowledge is a critical point that cannot be emphasized enough. In the West, emphasis and priority has been placed on intellectual knowing, for the most part to the exclusion of other means of knowing. The Taoists placed much emphasis on the body as a source of knowledge" (1128). At Equinox, this connection is stressed in the Staff Handbook:

> Increasing amounts of research are revealing the benefits of mindfulness in education and the importance of developing a mind-body connection in children from a young age. The holistic curriculum emphasizes a natural connection between body and mind. Students are encouraged to explore connections between their body and emotions and to develop an understanding of

what their bodies have to say. Each technique focuses on different aspects of the connection between mind and body. At Equinox, many teachers both practice and teach a wide range of mind-body approaches which include mindfulness meditation, creative visualization, drama, role-play, dance, yoga, Qi Gong, Focusing, and Brain Gym. Like all aspects of the holistic curriculum, there is growth and variation from year to year. The goal is for children to experience balance in their lives through the connection between mind and body. (EHAS 2017/2018, 6)

In the morning circles, students often do yoga or qigong exercises. In the study I did, almost every teacher used some form of meditation or mindfulness activity. One teacher had the students lead the daily meditation. The teacher introduced the idea of meditation then the students would take the lead. For example, he suggested focusing on the breath or a sound. He said:

> They look forward to it. It is a great segue into calming and focusing when coming in from outside. During the morning circle we do it along with many other things, tai chi, yoga, some drama. We do games from yoga such as the downward dog, where they have to hold the pose. They get imaginative where they can integrate their learning into games. (Miller 2016, 294)

One of the teachers had been doing mindfulness practices for years and it had become integral to his teaching. He said:

> We start with meditation and do mindful movements outside. We try to do noble silence. Coming in after lunch we do one minute. I also incorporate it into the health curriculum. I notice too when there is stress like before Christmas and Halloween. So we do guided meditations then. We will lie on the ground for about ten minutes. I also use it for being attentive, mindful listening. (Miller 2016, 295)

One of the students in this teacher's class suffered from obsessive compulsive disorder (OCD). He and his parents commented that the mindfulness was helpful to him and lowered his stress level. The father said, "It was wonderful. His OCD improved a lot."

Soul connections. "The spirit is where knowledge gathers; when the spirit is clear, knowledge is illumined. Knowledge is the seat of the heart" (Steiner 1976, 181). Spirit/soul is a defining characteristic of holistic education. In defining the holistic curriculum, I have stressed connections and relationships as the main vehicle for realizing the student's true nature. This is in keeping with Rudolf Steiner's (1976) suggestion that "moving from one thing to another in a way that connects one thing with another is more beneficial than anything else for the development of spirit and soul and even body" (173). It is also possible to directly connect students with their inner life, or their soul (Miller 2000). The soul is defined here as a vital and mysterious energy that gives meaning and purpose to one's life. In my book *Education and the Soul* (2000), I have described my understanding of soul and how it can be nurtured in students, our schools, and ourselves. Many of the approaches discussed in the other connections also nurture the soul (e.g., Earth connections, community connections).

At Equinox, the connections to the soul are outlined in the Staff Handbook:

> Connecting to the soul is central to the holistic approach at Equinox. The soul can be defined as *a vital and mysterious energy that gives meaning and purpose to one's life.* Time and guidance are offered for open-minded inquiry into the invisible. Singing and music are obvious ways to connect to the soul. Less obvious is oral storytelling and the telling of myths, legends and fairy tales from around the world – these stories connect us to our universal soul. These stories capture children's imaginations and nurture a deep connection to age-old stories that have been passed down through all cultures and throughout time. Daily classroom routines and rituals as well as school-wide celebrations also help to connect children to the soul. The honouring and creation of rituals around the natural cycles and processes present in the natural world not only have a soul connection but also deepen the connection to nature. (EHAS 2017/2018, 7, emphasis in original)

These connections are supported through the arts, such as performing a play every year. For several years, the primary students participated in *A Midsummer Night's Dream*. One teacher talked about how a student grew through the experience of being in the play:

> In primary we have done *A Midsummer Night's Dream* for five years. Also, we did a musical for junior level. We created a safe environment so it was not about

who got the main part. Saw real growth in students. One girl wanted to perform a particular role and at first I could not see her in that role. She was special [education and had ADD, attention deficit disorder]. She struggled with memory. She blew me away. She put her heart and soul into it.

Another teacher described a meditation activity that the students did before the holiday season:

> At holiday time, we had parents come too and we did a meditation around eating brown rice. We set up an altar with the rice on it. People reflected on the experience and were finding the world in their little rice. The bonding that happened was amazing. A transpersonal experience. We were connected. The kids and I know that we have been together in a special way. For 20–30 minutes there was silence. (Miller 2016, 295)

This experience has a Taoist tone. "Specifically, in a meditative state, one taps into the physical, spiritual and information state of all beings. One is connected with the Tao" (Yang, Lin, and Culham 2019, 1126).

Conclusion

In chapter 5 I discussed yin and yang and the concept of balance, which is another principle of holistic education. This balance is fluid, as yin and yang interact to move towards some form of harmony. In sum, then, holistic education is *inclusive* in its approach to teaching, fosters a variety of *connections*, and nurtures *balance* and harmony. Edward Slingerland (2014), a Taoist scholar whom I cited in chapter 4, writes from a Taoist perspective that "education should be analog, *holistic*, and oriented towards action" (213, my emphasis). Holistic education and the holistic curriculum as manifested at the Equinox Alternative Holistic School can help us provide the kind of education that Slingerland is advocating and that Taoist wisdom supports.

Chapter Seven

Yin and Yang: Play in Kindergarten and the Teachers' Role

Tian Ruan

When I hear, I forget. When I see, I remember. When I do, I understand.

Ancient Chinese Saying

My first contact with Taoism was when I was around five. I spent a summer with my grandpa who is a Taoist. I watched my grandpa practising qigong and meditating every day. I was so curious about what he was doing exactly because he looked so calm with his eyes closed. I tried to mimic him by closing my eyes and sitting like a "buddha" but could not sit still for over ten seconds. Grandpa laughed and he would have liked to tell me more, but I got distracted by other things easily and ran away.

I did not even notice that Taoism was embedded in my life and culture and that it has had an impact on education until I took the course Holistic Curriculum taught by John Miller in the summer of 2019. He asked students to meditate every day for five weeks. We were required to keep a journal that focused on how the process of meditation was going. After weeks of meditation practice, I generally experienced a sense of peace and harmony. I let go of troubling thoughts and was less concerned about problems in my life. Meditation lessened the peaks and valleys and gave me a more general sense of contentment. Self-cultivation which can include contemplation and meditation is an important part of Taoist practice, so meditating was my first real encounter with Taoist practices.

Maxwell King (2018) wrote that Fred Rogers (discussed in chapter 6) had stated that one of the major goals of education is to help students discover a greater awareness of their unique selves (328). This is also a major goal of a Taoist education. I want to find the balance between the whole and the part and to create lessons for young children within a larger vision of holistic education.

Yin and Yang in Kindergarten

The concepts of yin and yang are central to Taoism and Chinese philosophy. The character "yin" originally meant negative, the dark side where there is no sunlight. The character "yang" originally meant positive, the bright side where the sun shines. The traditional view is that yin and yang represent basic opposing forces within everything.

According to the *I Ching,* all things in the universe that are stable must have at least two opposing elements interconnected. Everything can reach a relatively stable state and a dynamic equilibrium because of having yin and yang at the same time. Yin and yang also represent a concept of dualism, describing how seemingly opposite or contrary forces can be complementary, interconnected, and interdependent in nature, and how they may give rise to each other as they interrelate with one another. Yin and yang can be applied to different areas of human behaviour. The concepts can inform educators and allow for the ability to shift perspectives and make adjustments when circumstances change (Chan 1963, 14–48). For example, if the teacher senses that there is too much yang in her classroom, she can make the adjustment to bring in more yin into the learning environment.

Early childhood education is important as it helps shape the life and growth of children and influences the development of their personalities, behaviours, and cognitive development. Believing in the concept that young children are naturally good and active learners, Friedrich Froebel opened the first kindergarten in Blankenburg, Germany, in 1837. He also believed this stage is crucial as it introduces the young learners to the education process while preparing them for other subsequent stages of life. Life is a continuous and consistent learning process. During children's early education, teachers and parents need to ensure the development of the whole child – head, hands, and heart. Froebel also believed in the importance of play for young children.

However, opportunities for children to engage in play are being eliminated in many schools because playing is seen as a waste of time. In the report *Crisis in the Kindergarten*, Edward Miller and Joan Almon (2009) wrote, "In an increasing number of kindergartens, teachers must follow scripts from which they may not deviate. These practices, which are not well-grounded in research, violate long-established principles of child development and good teaching" (1). The main argument of the report claims that play must be restored to foster genuine learning of the children. The research cited by Miller and Almon showed to what extent parents and teachers misunderstand "play" and the obstacles to play.

I agree with the main argument of the report that play can be both fun and educational. As a former kindergarten teacher and a current Mandarin teacher, I always believe that play is a learning tool, which ensures that children learn maximally while facilitating their holistic growth. Good play flourishes when children are allowed to engage in open-ended and imaginative activity, and when they are given the time to explore, experiment, and represent their growing understanding of the world. Kindergartners need a balance of child-centred play in the presence of teachers who help guide rather than direct learning. However, many teachers do not have a way of incorporating play in the classroom. Through play, children can construct new knowledge from the various toys that they use while playing. In their play, children express various behaviours and responses to their activity. For instance, if a toy is broken or if blocks they are using to build something fall down, children can express the feeling of anger but they will also try to repair their toy or reassemble the blocks so that they can function and use them again (Strasser and Mufson Koeppel 2010, 14). Through this, children acquire important knowledge such as problem-solving skills as they come to understand that despite the challenges that occur, they can seek solutions to these challenges.

Children during their early years in school are creative as they try new things. Teachers can find a balance between play and learning. Hands-on exploration and play are the primary ways young children learn, and block play is a wonderful example (Miller and Almon 2009). The block area is a standard learning area in kindergarten classrooms since blocks are ideal for learning. I enjoy seeing the harmony that block playing brings into the classroom. I consider playing yang because the children are building, creating, and laughing during the play. I believe learning as yin because it happens after playing and includes reflection. When children are learning through blocks, we might see them observing, using all of their senses, questioning, exploring, imagining, and recreating. We might hear them generating questions, making predictions, sharing and discussing thoughts and ideas with each other, and using new vocabulary. In the classroom, students are yang – they come to learn and absorb knowledge. While teachers are yin as learning through play is supported when they listen and respond to what children say. Teachers guide rather than direct. We help children to articulate their thoughts and support their oral language development.

Well-prepared teachers not only provide engaging interactions but also a safe, diverse, and positive classroom environment that supports learning. Physically, the classroom should have special structures that accommodate the creativity of the children as well as space to move freely during play without much disturbance from the surrounding environment. The space in a classroom for block play is critical since children will be doing constructive play where larger complex structures are made and many children are working together. In my classroom, the block space must be large enough to accommodate play. A large carpet area is a good place for story time gathering and major building projects. There are large hollow blocks, ramps, boards, unit blocks (as many shapes and sizes as possible, wooden or foam) and props: animals, food, human figures. During the play, kids can see shapes, quantities, sizes, colours as well as feel the materials. There are so many new vocabularies that I can teach them naturally. The combinations of different blocks allow children to integrate all their new experiences into their rapidly developing minds, bodies, and emotions. Sometimes children may seek out a change of stimuli – scenery, textures, colours, sounds, and smells. As children spend more time in one program, the more variation and stimulation are needed. Thus, I change pictures of different styles of architecture from around the world weekly and put on different selections of soft music when they are playing.

In addition, teachers need to understand the individual differences exhibited by different children within the classroom (Olds 2001, 12). These differences include mental, emotional, and physical differences that result in differentiated levels of learning. While growing up in China, a country that puts a strong emphasis on standardized testing, I did perform well in the testing, but I also lost the joy of learning. As I become a teacher, I want to focus on learning, particularly natural, organic learning processes. Instead of stressing a competitive, grade-driven process of evaluation that leads to students becoming "obedient to the authority of government and economic leaders" (Spring 1999, 53), the Tao promotes cooperation and encouragement. Thus, I want to create a balance between play and learning and assessing their growth. I try to include all students by fostering a safe learning environment. It is the role of the teacher to ensure flexible teaching and different learning materials for the children to accommodate their differences (Dombro, Jabion, and Stetson 2011, 105). For example, teachers can display images of children's building projects, finished or not, in the block play area. In my third plan, we talk about home and families, so I display pictures of every child in the program and their families. Considering diversities, other pictures on display include single-parent families, grandparent families, families with two-moms or two-dads, and homes of every race and ethnicity, including interracial and multiethnic families. Visual images are an important part of developing a feeling of belonging for all children, so the pictures of their families will help make connections to play.

My goal is for children to be exposed to the rich diversity of the entire world. Thus, I aim to create an environment of trust and respect. It is not easy to achieve, but it is achievable and worth the effort. I work hard at including all students so that everyone can see that I respect all views, not just a select few. I love this quote from the *International Handbook of Holistic Education* (Miller et al. 2019): "Holistic education doesn't merely dispense knowledge; it does so in a way that both the teacher and the student's soul is engaged and benefits" (xxv). My play plan is like a bridge that connects every child and teacher, not only letting students explore themselves and be with others but also allows the teacher to understand each individual and build a loving, spiritual community. Moreover, it can be done through multicultural artwork, photos, and signs in different languages on the wall and books, music, and artefacts in the play area. In their article, "The Effects of Stereotyped Toys and Gender on Play Assessment in Children Aged 18–47 Months," Cherney et al. (2003) wrote that teachers and other education facilitators should also tailor the playing materials to ensure they incorporate the socialization and gender aspects of respective children (95).

One way I tailor playing materials is by using stickers as learning tools and artefacts in the play area. Children like stickers because they like collecting things and they like using them for self-expression. Stickers can represent many associations that children can work with. Thus, I carefully select stickers that represent different races, genders, and occupations. I always ask my students to combine several stickers and create a sentence or even a story, and I use these examples as a teaching moment. For example, once Nolan, a student, chose a Disney princess sticker and a helicopter sticker. He was frustrated with these two stickers. As I encourage boys in my class to talk about their feelings and worries, I found out that Nolan was having difficulty connecting the two stickers in a way that would create a story. I wanted to avoid introducing a gender stereotype like a typical fairy tale that a princess would live in a castle and be saved by a prince. Instead, I encouraged him to think about how a princess can be whoever she wants to be if she puts effort into training and practise.

I helped him create the story that told how the master pilot taught the princess how to fly a helicopter; they had several training sessions and finally she formed a team of princess pilots. It is important to avoid gender and social stereotypes. Thus, good use of playing materials can extend learning opportunities and the teachers can grow with the students and explore their imaginative world together. Children learn important social, emotional, and physical life skills through play. It is important to avoid gender and social stereotypes starting in early childhood, so I provide children of both genders with books and images that feature non-traditional gender roles such as female astronauts, athletes, and scientists and male teachers, dancers, and nurses. Playing with a variety of toys and images provide opportunities to develop and extend learning opportunities so that the teachers can grow with the students and explore their imaginative world together.

I created a block play plan that consists of three different approaches to improving children's learning and development. I believe that the development is holistic, which means mental, social, emotional, and spiritual variables are interconnected in a child's life. Thus, progress in one area affects progress in others. Similarly, when something goes wrong in any one of those areas, it has an impact on all the other areas. Understanding this, I used my intuition to know when to bring in more *yin* or more *yang* into the classroom. In the following pages, I would like to share my block plans, the reflections I had after teaching each lesson, and the rationale of the whole plan.

Block Play Plans

Students' grades: JK and SK
Background: It's an after-school Mandarin language program in Toronto. There are ten students and they are beginning Mandarin learners. The teacher communicates with students in Mandarin but may use English to explain some instructions. Students are encouraged to speak Mandarin as much as possible.

Activity focuses on development in the following areas:

1. Creativity: Blocks can be moved freely to be combined in countless ways.
2. Motor skills: Children use their hands and fingers to move blocks and manipulate small objects.
3. Imagination: Children can follow their interests to create something new.
4. Logical thinking: Children ask themselves, Why do I build in this way and how does this connect to the real-life situation?
5. Problem-solving: Children ask themselves how to solve a problem.
6. Self-expression: Children discover that they have ideas and they can bring their ideas to life.
7. Social and language growth: Children learn to take turns to talk about their buildings and share thoughts while using new Mandarin vocabulary, phrases, and sentences.

Preparatory experiences for the play include children having experiences with building blocks. For example, they combine the blocks to make complex structures. Children also begin to share ideas and learn to be a respectful listener when it is the other person's turn to share. They also know how to use an iPad to read and draw.

Physical settings and materials include a large, open area for circle and story time with most tables placed around the carpet. There are large hollow blocks, ramps, and boards. The blocks usually have as many shapes and sizes as possible and are made of wood or foam. There are also cardboard, metal, or plastic tubes as well as various props: animals, food, human figures, natural materials, construction tools. Finally, there are pictures and iPads.

See the appendix at the end of this chapter for the three plans and a list of resources.

Block Play Type 1

Block play is typically found in classrooms for younger children. It lends itself to so many skills, including imagining and creating, developing math concepts, and even second-language learning. When the building is done, the children can practise cleaning up and being responsible for their environment.

I initially use a competition to get the children involved and to build their confidence. Whether working alone or as a group, children feel proud of their accomplishments, like building a bridge that spans the block area, a ramp that works, or a towering multilevel building. For the teacher, it is a good opportunity to teach social and emotional skills. My little block builders learn to follow classroom safety rules, to respect the rights of others, and to stand up for their rights. I encourage them to use language like 谢谢 (thank you), 请 (please),and 不客气 (you are welcome) when we practise being respectful and showing care for the classroom environment. In order to build tall and complex structures that don't topple over, children apply principles of architecture and engineering, such as stable bases and balanced structures. I am always impressed by these kindergarteners using their thinking skills to negotiate and resolve conflicts; it is also a good time to help them expand their Mandarin vocabulary.

As I teach, I find block play can develop the children's persistence and engagement with some prompts. Initially, many children consider their structures to be complete after only ten minutes; but, with my prompts, they are able to refocus and continue building for an extended time. Children work with the building materials as well as small animals or people figures, which change the narrative to include characters' actions. The addition of these figures help to sustain less engaged builders, providing renewed inspiration to continue building.

Kathy is the girl who is passionate about everything but has a short attention span. During block play, she builds something quickly and loses interest soon after she is finished. In order to motivate her again, I bring some toy animals, figures, and stickers to her and give her the task to decorate each floor of her building. I tell her she can invite anyone to live in her building so she needs to decorate each floor in a way that each person likes. Kathy starts to think who she wants to invite and what they like, so she becomes re-engaged in the play for another twenty minutes.

I learn a lot from children by watching them play. I take anecdotal notes and document their activities. Teachers who describe the children's actions while they are engaged in block play are helping the children develop receptive and expressive language. Thus, I ask open-ended questions to encourage more conversation and opportunities to expand on the children's thought process. During building time, I consistently ask questions such as the following:

- 你还要再增加什么吗? (Would you like to bring in something else?)
- 什么会让你的建筑更有趣呢? (What would be interesting to add?)
- 我观察了你搭了这个. 如果加上 … 会发生什么呢? (I notice that you built this up. I wonder what would happen if you …)
- 你的建筑有多高? (How many blocks high is that structure?)
- 有比你的朋友还高吗? (Is that taller than your friend?)

Overall, block play is fundamental to the growth and development of children and can be a part of every child's experience throughout the early years.

Block Play Type 2

Play is a joy that most children instinctively engage in. By using imagination, make-believe play allows children to have control over their world. The second form of play is constructive and creative. It happens when children use objects or toys to create something; in this case, children are building zoos. My kindergarteners started to understand how the blocks fit together and tried to create elaborate structures.

This second form of play involves reading out loud with related block play. Here imagination is yin and realistic thinking is yang. In order to achieve the harmony of the play, the children not only use imagination to build a zoo but also think about the real-world situation and what environments different animals live in. Block play encourages children to match, count, and sort. While watching a child playing with blocks or co-playing with another child, I take advantage of the opportunity to teach Mandarin vocabulary, introducing words to describe the shapes of the blocks (rectangles, squares, and triangles) as well as the colours and number of blocks. I introduce new vocabulary and the meaning of opposites, such as more and less, big and small, half and whole, and so on.

As mentioned before, the teacher is yin and the students are yang. The play is not controlled by adults, but as a teacher, I am involved a lot during the play. The interaction between children and teachers in child-driven play helps improve communication and bonding. At the beginning of block play, I ask what each child wants to build and help him/her to devise a plan. During block play, without doing the construction for the child, I continue to ask questions such as, "Do you think it is going to stay balanced?" and "Do you want to make space for a door?" and "What do you think a penguin may need?" These questions encourage the child to continue to think and create. Block play can help children learn social skills as they work together with other children. The discussion at the end of block play allows them to explore, cooperate, and create a story that includes everyone in the class. By the end of the class, the children have come up with a story. The story is that I take them on a field trip to the zoo on a sunny day, where Cate (one of the children in the class whose zoo got the most compliments from other friends) is the zookeeper. Everyone adopts an animal in the story and are happy with their animals. During the telling of the story, I am impressed by how many details each friend contributes to make the story so vivid. In addition, we review a lot of Mandarin vocabulary that relates to animals in the zoo. Such play that cultivates conversation and storytelling among friends builds the foundation for a child's imagination to move with ease beyond the immediate circumstances. Enhancing yin and yang balance is done by giving enough space mentally and physically to the children in the classroom. It allows them to use their imagination as well as discover self-values and self-interests; they may understand themselves better and become more independent.

Block Play Type 3

"The home should be the treasure chest of living," said Le Corbusier, the renowned Swiss-French architect.

For most children, their home is just such a treasure chest, as well as the setting of many adventures. It is also their introduction to architecture, and can leave a lasting impression that will influence how they view their world. Drawing pictures and sharing on the iPad, provides a different way to create art pieces. Those pictures are saved as documentation and are sent immediately to the parents. One of the main purposes of this type of play is for children to think about their home and family. Parents provide the basic physical necessities and emotional care for their children. A home is a place where they can feel cozy and safe.

This form of play connects to social studies and involves drawing and building blocks; however, it also requires children to think and recall what their homes look like in detail. They need to build their homes accordingly and share them with their friends. It is a good opportunity to practise the children's language skills as well as for the teacher and children to get to know each other better. I talk about different houses all around the world, how different climates and cultures affect housing and individual roles in each family. I share a picture of my family and home in Shanghai, China, with the class. Many of my students have Asian roots but have not been to the East. Some children were surprised that my home in Shanghai was not made of stones like the Great Wall but looked like a "normal" apartment building. I take this moment as an opportunity to introduce 全球化 (globalization) to them and explain that things used to be very different in Eastern and Western countries, but now countries and people of the world are interacting and becoming more integrated. I also tell my students that they are learning Mandarin so they can better communicate with people from the other side of the world. This brings up an interesting class discussion about their relatives who live in China and what their lives there must be like, including whether they speak Cantonese or Mandarin. Later, we talk about the changes in the family structure in China. Sharing things about my home and family help build trust between myself and the children. During the discussion on individual responsibilities at home, I use appropriate vocabulary since the kindergarteners are too young and their Mandarin level is not strong enough to generate conversation on their own. We finally conclude that in strong, functional families, every member learns how to love and accept love, be effective communicators, and be responsible citizens. I assign homework after the class, which is to hug their family members and tell them "I love you." They need to teach their family to say "I love you" in Mandarin, too.

Rationale

Yin and yang should interact to create wholeness. Jing Lin (2006) describes these two qualities as "yang is the energy that creates and motivates and yin is the energy that nourishes, nurtures, sustains and harmonizes ... the balance of yang and yin preconditions the harmonious existence of nature and human beings" (80). In chapter 5, Miller writes about the classroom in terms of yin and yang, as illustrated in Table 5.1. I reproduce the table here (Table 7.1) and discuss a few of the elements below.

Individual/Group: My first type of block play served as the introduction to the whole plan, beginning with a block building competition. Announcing the competition worked as a "hook" to get children interested. With the competition, children were excited as they tried to outdo their classmates. However, I wanted to maintain the balance between being independent and interdependent in my classroom. It was also a good time to educate them about the rules of playing with toys and appropriate behaviour working with other students who want to join the play. Vivian Gussin Paley, who was a kindergarten teacher and early childhood education researcher, worked hard to actively involve all the students in the class. She would even pick the child that was often left out so they felt included. In *You Can't Say You Can't Play*, Paley (2003) used several stories, including "Magpie and Raymond," to explain rejection and loneliness that students go through. She used the same stories to bring the students together and engage them in classwork, and she inspired me to use stories to bring everyone together.

Table 7.1. Balance between Yang and Yin in the Curriculum and the Classroom

Yang	Yin
Individual	Group
Content	Process
Knowledge	Imagination
Rational	Intuitive
Quantitative Assessment	Qualitative Assessment
Techniques/Strategies	Vision
Assessment/Evaluation	Instruction/Learning
Technology	Program
Whole	Part

Source: Miller (2019b, 10–12).

Through the stories, students feel the emotion each character experiences since they learn to put themselves in that situation. The "no rejecting rule" Paley made is a seed that can be planted in students' minds.

A good holistic plan should never leave out any difficult topics. My third plan talks about family and home so the teacher can teach students to embrace differences and diversity. When teaching "family," teachers may deal with difficult topics like immigration, divorce, LGBTQ+ families, and death. We need to teach our students to be capable and strong (traditionally masculine qualities) and how to remain yielding and calm (traditionally feminine qualities). Taoism embraces the feminine. When teaching, we should be aware of the masculine/feminine duality. *Wen-tzu* elaborates on the importance of the feminine, "Because they keep to the feminine, they can establish the masculine ... Being as a female to the world, they are able to avoid spiritual death" (quoted in Cleary 2003c, 186). Feminine here is "a women's care." It was important to talk about and listen to every child's feelings when these events happened. Of equal value are the personal gains acquired by students when they learn stories from their cultural backgrounds and from other cultures as well. My purpose is to help each student to see the world through someone else's eyes, to learn to understand other people's circumstances and perspectives, and to empathize with them. Although every individual is unique, we come together and can gradually form a strong, whole group.

Knowledge/Imagination: Curiosity is a major characteristic in young children. Through block building, children can satisfy their curiosity and imagination. I believe every child is a good storyteller. During the read-aloud time, Shira, a four-year-old in my class volunteered to read aloud *Goodnight Gorilla* (Mandarin version) to the class. I was glad that she was so brave to do so, but I also felt a bit worried. She could barely read in English, so how could she read a book in Mandarin? She took the book and started to read. After listening, it dawned on me that she could use her imagination. She looked at each picture and created an even more interesting story that she wanted to tell. Although the new story was different from the original one, it made sense. When another child, Ammar, was playing with a toy car, he imagined he was flying an airplane. His airplane story was so detailed except the airplane looked like a car. Imagination is a way for children to create their own reality and develop their own reasons to support that reality.

Assessment/Learning: In the third plan, which moves from fantasy to the real world, children use blocks to build the house/apartment where they live. Before the block play, they took turns to share where they lived and how many family members they had living with them. During their play, I would come around and ask questions about how many floors there were in the house, how many bedrooms they had, and what their room looked like. After playing, I encouraged them to share their favourite thing they did at home. Language plays a particularly important role because it is one of the most important ways for the teacher to understand and assesses how students are thinking (Michaels, Shouse, and Schweingruber 2008, 88). Talking allows students to think and articulate ideas. At the same time, it is also important to include space and silence. The role of a teacher is to join a group, be a good listener, and show care and emotional support. I also believe the teacher should share things about his/her own home and family as this helps the teacher connect to the students. All this gives children even more confidence in class discussions.

Reason/Intuition: All human beings are multidimensional, with conscious and unconscious aspects, and rational and intuitive thinking. In the early years, the holistic approach helps a child in motor development, cognitive development, and socio-emotional development. It is a holistic approach that calls for a merging of reason and intuition. These two elements are necessary for the development of the child (Olds 2001). The block play enriches thinking, which allows children to come up with new vocabulary, shapes, and imaginative structures that contribute to learning.

The traditional ways of learning a second language can be teacher-centred, such as using flashcards to memorize words and reading the textbook. Young children can sometimes try too hard to grasp the skill or concept that results in frustration and giving up. However, I incorporate block play with a lot of literacy elements to promote learning Mandarin. Block play fosters creativity, fine motor skills, and logical thinking. I have also been inspired by Gillian Dowley McNamee's (2015) book *The High-Performing Preschool: Story Acting in Head Start Classrooms*, which stresses the importance of storytelling and imagination. In it she writes that "pretend play that cultivates conversation and storytelling among friends builds the foundation for a child's imagination to move with ease beyond the immediate circumstances" (139). Every plan involves read-aloud time and related block play, and I provide a lot of picture books in the classroom library for the children to look at and read.

The Balance/Relationship between Teachers and Students

I grew up in China and came to North America to further studies after finishing high school, so I have experienced both Eastern and Western educational approaches as a student and a teacher. As a result, I want to find balance in my class. One of the most obvious differences between Eastern and Western settings is seen when a teacher asks students for their opinions or to give their thoughts on a passage they have read, or to express new ideas for resolving an issue. When I was a student at Penn State University and then the Ontario Institute for Studies in Education at the University of Toronto, professors usually encouraged us as students to express, discuss, or even debate openly and freely. This is in contrast to Eastern teaching styles that generally provide little opportunity for free thinking or analysis.

Amy Dombro, Jabion, and Stetson (2011) point out vividly the importance of interactions of children in the classroom as they learn from their peers during arguments, negotiations, and discussions. According to these authors, powerful interactions have three steps: be present, connect, and extend learning (4). These steps emphasize the need to involve children in activities and to include the quieter ones to enhance their thinking capacity. Providing opportunities for play allows children to satisfy their desires to create, dramatize, and tell stories. This helps them identify the interests they want to pursue.

Dombro, Jabion, and Stetson (2011) wrote, "In the rich teaching moment, you stay present, so that you can intentionally make sensitive and responsive decisions about the individual child's learning needs" (70). Block play helps develop children's persistence and engagement. Initially, many children may consider their structures to be complete after only ten minutes, but with their teacher's prompts, children can refocus and continue building for an extended time. The second form of block play requires children to build a zoo by using imagination and knowledge. I move around the classroom and help the children with questions. I also acknowledge the children who have built creative blocks. Angeline Lillard (2013), in "Playful Learning and Montessori Education," writes that giving a child a compliment not only encourages the child but also increases his/her confidence in other activities (164). Teachers should also be cautious of the negative facial expressions that they show when some of the children make mistakes when building with their blocks. Teachers need to allow the children to exercise the creativity and imagination in play without reprimanding them but only guiding them when necessary. Children need to have control in order to achieve the benefits of play. The interaction between children and teachers in child-driven play helps improve the connection between teacher and student.

Conclusion

A basic principle of the Tao, the concept of balance, can be achieved through yin and yang in teaching and learning. The teacher can learn to balance activities that require analysing information in "linear ways (*yang*)" with other activities that involve "creativity, emotional expression, and personal insight (*yin*)" (Nagel 1994, 125). My different approaches to play are designed not only to ensure genuine learning but also to make learning enjoyable and fun. Giving space mentally and physically to children allows them to use imagination as well as discover self-values and self-interests. They may understand themselves better and become more independent. Students can learn from having a balance of both yin and yang experiences. Early childhood education forms a baseline for the children as they will be introduced to higher levels of learning as they progress through school. As mentioned before, opportunities for children to engage in play are being eliminated in many schools. In the report *Crisis in the Kindergarten*, Miller and Almon (2009) write, "In an increasing number of kindergartens, teachers must follow scripts from which they may not deviate. These practices, which are not well-grounded in research, violate long-established principles of child development and good teaching" (11). Students at young ages need a balance of child-centred play and focused learning guided by the teacher.

My lessons are play-based, and are represented in three block play plans that provide safe and conducive surroundings for young learners and, at the same time, enable social, intellectual, physical, emotional, and spiritual development. Good play flourishes when children are allowed to engage in open-ended, imaginative activity and are given the time to explore, experiment, and represent their growing understanding of the world. When interest is high, the substance is easily retained. Positive motivation is critical in promoting deep and lasting learning. Learning is increased by day-to-day effort, but growing in the Tao can occur in effortless ways through play. As much as possible, learning should occur naturally. At the end of a successful day, the good learner and the teacher can feel that all things flowed. Play is both fun and educational.

Appendix to Chapter 7

Block Play Plan 1

Focus: Problem-solving, imagination, and self-expression

Anticipated events

Tell the children that we are going to have a building block competition.

1. Show the children the video, "The Top 20 Most Amazing and Strangest Buildings around the World."
2. Explain the rules (thirty minutes for building time; after building, the children will have sharing time; and then they will vote for the winner). Please be as creative as you can.
3. Talk about manners when building (gently, friendly, sharing, etc.).
4. Have a stopwatch and begin when the children are ready.
5. When time is up, tell the children to stop and share what they have built one by one.
6. Respond to children's language and build on their ideas and interests.
7. After all the children have shared, ask them to share one thing they like about other children's buildings.
8. Let children vote for the "most interesting" and "fanciest" building.
9. After finishing the buildings, the teacher can engage the children in discussions about the buildings by making connections with the stories that have been read to them. For example, books such as *The Three Little Pigs* can inspire discussions about structurally sound buildings.
10. Ask children to quietly clean up, and the winner will get a sweet treat as a prize.

Accommodations for differences among children (language, ability, personality)

1. Play soft music when the children are playing.
2. If a child does not want to share what he/she built verbally, he/she can draw a picture.

3. Provide children with frequently used sentence structures when they share ideas. For example: 我喜欢 … 因为 …. One thing I like about ___'s building is _____ because _____.
4. Remind children how many minutes they have left.

Block Play Plan 2

Focus: Logic thinking, imagination, and self-expression

Linkage to Plan 1

Plan 2 builds from plan 1. Since plan 1 was about building whatever children want, plan 2 has a specific topic that the children focus on. In plan 1, students have some sharing time about what they built, while plan 2 has them practising language skills and allows them to talk more during the discussion. Both plan 1 and plan 2 enable children to express and use their imagination, but from different perspectives. Plan 1 allows the children to use fantasy while plan 2 allows them to build both ideal and realistic architectures.

Anticipated events

Tell the children they are going to build a zoo.

1. Ask the children to share experiences of visiting a zoo.
2. Read aloud the book *If I Ran a Zoo* by Dr. Seuss in Mandarin.
3. Talk about what animals live in a zoo, and what they need, what kind of environment they live in.
4. Talk about manners when building (gently, friendly, sharing, etc.).
5. When the children are building their zoos, ask what kind of zoo they are building, what animals are there in the zoo, how many zookeepers there are and so on to prompt thinking.
6. Ask the children to build a zoo that relates to the real world as different animals need different environments. For example, penguins and polar bears need ice. Pandas need bamboo. Wolves need spaces to run.
7. Respond to the children's language and build on their ideas and interests.

8. After all the children share, ask them about one favourite thing they like from another child's zoo.
9. After cleaning up, let the children read other books about zoos on their own or they can just relax on the carpet.

Accommodations for differences among children
(language, ability, personality)

1. When reading aloud to children, keep reading slowly and use pictures to help students understand better.
2. During the discussion, they can draw pictures to help explain the zoo to others.
3. The teacher can print out a word bank of animals with pictures in both English and Mandarin and place them beside the children. If they do not know the animal in Mandarin, they can show the cards.
4. Print out a visual activity schedule with pictures and simple words explaining the plan.

Block Play Plan 3

Focus: Logical thinking, motor skill, storytelling, language development

Linkage to Plans 1 and 2

All of the three plans are about building blocks, but each has a different focus and purpose. The first form of play is creating buildings. The second form is building a zoo, which allows children to think about reality while being creative as well. The third type of play moves from fantasy to the real world as the children will use the blocks to build a model of the house/ apartment where they live.

Through the whole plan, children will start with a general introduction to architecture, and gradually move to a special focus. They will be aware of the diverse buildings around the world, and that every single home is different. Plan 3 adds the important values of embracing differences and being a responsible family member, which brings the lesson to a higher level.

Anticipated events

Read aloud the book *Come Over to My House* by Theo LeSieg in Mandarin.

1. Talk about housing styles through history and different cultures. Show pictures and the video, "Classic Sesame Street – Homes Around the World."
2. Ask the children to draw a picture of their home with their families using the Drawing Pad app on the iPad.
3. Ask the children to put their drawing into the Explain Everything app and talk about it there. Give everyone "Me time" to share where they live and how many family members they have.
4. Tell the children they are going to build their homes with blocks.
5. When children are building their homes, remind them to think about how many floors there are in their house, how many bedrooms, what their room look like, and so on to promote thinking.
6. Ask children to stop and to share what they have built one by one.
7. Encourage the children to share their favourite things to do at home.
8. Respond to the children's language and build on their ideas and interests.
9. After sharing, tell children that a home is a place where they feel cozy and safe, no matter where they live or how big the house is.
10. Talk about what matters most for building strong families and how important it is that all family members help each other to be well and succeed.

Accommodations for differences among children
(language, ability, personality)

1. When reading aloud to the children, keep reading slowly and use pictures as hints for kids to understand better.
2. The teacher can print out a word bank of houses, furniture, and family with pictures in both English and Mandarin and place them beside the children. If they do not know the word in Mandarin, they can show the cards.
3. Provide sentence structures for children in need. Print out a visual activity schedule with pictures and simple words explaining the plan for them.

4. Children may come from very different family backgrounds. For the children whose parents are divorced, the teacher may tell them all that sometimes home is not just one place. Encourage them to share, draw, and build what they like about Daddy's Home and Mommy's Home.

Resources for My Class

Technology: iPad with drawing pad and Explain Everything downloaded.

Children's books in the classroom library:

Come Over to My House by Theo LeSieg
The Little House by Virginia Lee Burton
Goodnight Moon by Margaret Wise Brown
Home by Carson Ellis
If You Lived Here: Houses of the World by Giles Laroche
How a House Is Built by Gail Gibbons
Two Homes by Claire Masurel
If I Ran a Zoo by Dr. Seuss
Goodnight Gorilla by Peggy Rathmann
Be Nice to Spiders by Margaret Bloy Graham
Don't Feed the Boy by Irene Lathman
Dear Zoo by Rod Campbell
Polar Bear, Polar Bear, What Do You Hear? by Bill Martin Jr. and Eric Carle
Put Me in the Zoo by Robert Lopshire
The Three Little Pigs

Chapter Eight

A New Vision for Education

Taoism and Indigenous wisdom offer ways that we can heal ourselves and the planet. Thomas Berry was a powerful voice in addressing ecological catastrophe through such books as *The Dream of the Earth*. In *The Dream of the Earth*, he calls for a New Story, an ecological age. "One of the main characteristics of the emerging ecological period is the move from a human-centered norm of reality and value to a nature centered norm" (Berry 1988, 161). Berry was influenced by three different sources: Chinese thought, Indigenous traditions, and the work of Pierre Teilhard de Chardin. As a young man, he was very interested in Confucianism and Taoism and went to China in 1948 to study Chinese. Mary Evelyn Tucker, John Grim, and Andrew Angyal (2019) in their recent biography of Berry discuss the influence of Chinese thought and the writing of Xunzi, who wrote, "Heaven, has its seasons: Earth has its resources; humans have their government" (234). They point out:

> He [Berry] frequently referred to the triad of Heaven, Earth, and humans as an interpenetrating cosmological worldview. He realized that modern Western philosophy and religion had left behind such an integrated worldview for a dualistic one that separated humans from nature and maintained a division between humans and the Divine as a transcendent being. (234)

In *The Dream of the Earth*, Berry (1988) cited the sixteenth-century scholar Wang Yang Ming who wrote about the connection between heaven, earth, humans, and all living things:

Everything from ruler, minister, husband, wife, and friends to mountains, rivers, heavenly and earthy spirits, birds, animals and plants; all should be truly loved in order to realize my humanity which forms a unity, and then my clear character will be completely manifested and I will really form one body between earth, and the myriad things. (15)

Berry saw Chinese philosophy as a vibrant tradition that helped him develop his view that saw the universe as an integrated whole where "humans can only attain their full humanity in relationship to both cosmos and Earth ... He was inspired throughout his life by the Confucian tradition and its articulation of such a cosmological, ecological and moral vision" (Tucker, Grim, and Angyal 2019, 239). Berry (1988) also referred to Taoism and its principles. He wrote, "The word, the self-spoken word, by its own spontaneities brought forth the universe and established itself as the ultimate norm of reality and of value. This is in accord with Lao-Tzu, the Chinese Sage, who tells us the human models itself on the earth, earth models itself on heaven, heaven models itself on tao, tao models itself on its own spontaneity" (196).

Berry (1988) recognized the importance of spontaneity in nature and the universe, "Our own actions can be truly creative only when they are guided by these deeper spontaneities" (48). Berry also wrote, "The natural world is the larger sacred community to which we belong" (81). Like the ancient Chinese, Berry saw humanity intimately connected to the unfolding of creation which "must now be experienced as the emergence of the universe as a psychic-spiritual as well as a material-physical reality from the beginning. We need to see ourselves as integral with this emergent process" (81). Berry believed that "spiritual discipline and spiritual experience" are integral to seeing ourselves as part the divine mystery of the universe and is part of the New Story.

Berry (1988) also argued that education has an important role to play in the New Story. He wrote, "Teaching children about the natural world should be treated as one of the most important events in their lives. Children need a story that will bring personal meaning together with the grandeur and meaning of the universe" (131). Central to the New Story and to education is seeing that "we bear the universe in our being as the universe bears us in its being" (131). Brian Swimme, Mary Ellen Tucker, and others have worked on developing curricula and learning materials that support this vision and the New Story. Swimme's work with Berry on *The Universe Story* (1992) and his more recent work with Mary Ellen Tucker on the *Journey of the Universe* (2011) allow students to see themselves as intimately connected to the universe's unfolding.

Karen Armstrong (2019) also cites the importance of Chinese thinkers in her most recent book and writes "there has been a growing conviction that the traditional Chinese cultivation of reverence for the cosmos may prove to be what the world really needs" (423). More specifically, she says contemporary Chinese scholars, including Qian Mu, Tang Junyi, and Feng Yulan, "have decided that the most significant contribution to the modern world that Confucianism can make is its ideal of the 'unity of Heaven and humanity' (*tianrenheyi*)." These scholars also "point out that human beings have evolved from 'Heaven' and are imbued with the same vital energy as stones, plants and animals" (480). They refer to the ancient text, *The Doctrine of the Mean*:

> The heaven now before us is only this bright, shining mass; but when viewed in its unlimited extent, the sun, moon, stars and constellations are suspended in it and all things are covered by it. The earth before us is but a handful of soil; but in its breadth and depth, it sustains mountains like Hua and Yueh without feeling their weight, contains the rivers and seas without letting them leak away, and sustains all things. The mountain before us is only a fistful of straw; but in all the vastness of its size, grass and trees grow upon it, birds and beasts dwell in it, and stores of precious things [minerals] are discovered in it. The water before us is but a spoonful of liquid, but in all its unfathomable depth, the monsters, dragons, fishes and turtles are produced in them, and wealth becomes abundant because of it. (quoted in Armstrong 2019, 480)

Armstrong (2019) suggests that we require "self-knowledge, introspection, and deep reflection" to come into harmony with the Earth and the cosmos. This includes contemplation and self-cultivation (discussed in chapter 3 of this book). The Chinese scholars mentioned above have endorsed the Earth Charter (29 June 2000) that must include "care for the community of life with understanding, compassion and love." Taoism and Confucianism can allow us to view the Earth and the cosmos as sacred. Tu Wieming has written, "We understand that what is regarded as sacred is more likely to be treated with care and respect. Our planetary home should be so regarded. Efforts to safeguard and cherish the environment need to be infused with a vision of the sacred" (Weiming and Tucker 2004, 497).

Both Berry and Armstrong cite the famous "Western Inscription" by Zhang Zai (1020–1077). It is called the "Western Inscription" because it was on the west wall of Zhang's study. It is a beautiful description of our connection to all things in the universe and the compassion that arises from the connection:

> Heaven is my father and earth is my mother, and even such small creature as I finds an intimate place in their midst.
>
> Therefore, that which extends through the universe I regard as my body and that which directs the universe I consider as my nature.
>
> All people are my brothers and sisters, and all things are my companions … Respect the aged – this is the way to treat them as elders should be treated. Show affection toward the orphaned and weak – this is the way to treat them as the young should be treated … Even those who are tired and infirm, crippled or sick, those who have no brothers or children, wives or husbands, are all my brothers who are in distress and have no one to turn to …
>
> In life, I follow and serve [Heaven and Earth]. In death, I will be at peace. (De Bary, Theodore, and Bloom 1999, 683–4)

This vision has been echoed throughout history and can be found in the Indigenous peoples writing as well as in the writings about love by Martin Luther King Jr. and Mahatma Gandhi. Richard Wagamese (2016) describes an Indigenous vision of how we are connected to everything:

> I've been considering the phrase "all my relations" for some time now. It's hugely important. It's our saving grace in the end. It points to the truth that we are all related, that we are all connected, that we all belong to each other. The most important word is "all." Not just those who look like me, sing like me, dance like me, speak like me, pray like me or behave like me. ALL my relations. That means every person, just as it means every rock, mineral, blade of grass, and creature. We live because everything else does. If we were to choose collectively to live

that teaching, the energy of our change of consciousness would heal each of us – and the planet. (36)

The vision of Indigenous Peoples had a powerful influence on Berry, which he included in *The Dream of the Earth* (1988) and his other works. Indigenous Peoples recognized the wisdom of Thomas Berry as well. He was invited to speak at Indigenous gatherings. At one meeting, Chief Tom Porter, an Elder of the Mohawk Kanastsiohareke community in upstate New York, "said in his speech that he had never heard a non-Indian speak so much like his grandfather and the older men of this memory. He turned and addressed Thomas as 'Grandfather'" (Tucker, Grim, and Angyal 2019, 243–4). Berry felt this was one of the most important moments in his life.

The other major influence on Thomas Berry was Pierre Teilhard de Chardin. Particularly important was Teilhard de Chardin's concept of cosmogenesis, which sees the universe as evolving. Human beings are part of the evolution and their self-reflective consciousness can help shape its evolution. For Berry, this was an important aspect of his vision of the new story and what he called the Great Work. Another important aspect of Teilhard de Chardin's vision was love. Teilhard de Chardin (1968) wrote, "For the first time in history humans have become capable not only of knowing and serving evolution but of loving it" (172). He went on to say that this "love" is the "second fire" that helps in the evolution of the cosmos. Today, Ilia Delio (2016) writes in the tradition of Teilhard de Chardin and continues to expand on the power of love:

What Teilhard suggests is that mysticism is at the heart of created life. We are held by an embrace of Love, a "love-field" sustaining us at every moment. This field of love is God, the hidden depth and core of being that makes wholeness of being possible. We must discover this love for the evolution of human life and this means coming home to ourselves and being at home within ourselves. (100)

Like Berry and Teilhard de Chardin, Delio (2016) writes about love in the context of nature. "We belong to one another because we have the same source of love; the love that flows through the trees is the same love that flows through my being ... We are deeply connected in this flow of love, beginning on the level of nature where we are the closest of kin because the earth is our mother" (180). And, she writes, "education plays a vital role in how we love" (163). I have written about the role of love in education and how it has many forms that need to be nourished in our classrooms and schools (Miller 2018). Some of these forms include self-love, impartial love, love of learning, love of beauty, cosmic love, and non-violence. King Jr. and Gandhi both practised non-violence and both wrote about how love is the most powerful force in the universe. King Jr. saw "love as the supreme unifying principle of life," and Gandhi wrote, "The force of love is the same as the force of the soul or truth. We have evidence of it working at every step. The universe would disappear without the existence of that force" (quoted in Nagler and Van Hook 2019, 67). Their belief in the power of universal love was the basis for much of the work they did to inspire positive social change.

The work of Gregory Cajete (1994) can help actualize the new vision, particularly his book *Look to the Mountain: An Ecology of Indigenous Education*. He writes, "With or without our conscious participation, *a new story of education is emerging* ... To begin such a process, American education must move from a focus on specialization to holistic knowledge; from a focus on structures to understanding processes, from objective science to systemic science and from building to networking" (41, my emphasis; 27). He describes the principles of Indigenous education, many of which are similar to the principles of Taoism and holistic education. Some of these include:

- A sacred view of Nature permeates its foundational process of teaching and learning.
- Integration and interconnectedness are universal traits of its contexts and processes.
- It recognizes that the true source of knowledge are found within the individual and the entities of Nature.
- It honours the ebb and flow of learning as it moves through individuals, community, Nature, and the cosmos.
- It uses story to root a perspective that unfolds through the special use of language.

...

- It recognizes that learning is about seeing the whole through the parts.
- We learn through our bodies and spirits as much as through our minds.

- Overt intellectualization is kept to a minimum in favour of direct experience and learning by doing.
- Tribal teachers realize that striving for real knowledge requires a cultivated sense of humility.
- The cultivation of humility prepares the student to learn the nature of attention. (Cajete 1994, 29–31, 224–7)

Cajete (1994) also writes that "meaning is seen in the natural world and its workings and that all things comprising Nature are teachers of mankind" (228). Cajete's book provides many examples of Indigenous and holistic learning.

Yang, Lin, and Culham (2019) make a strong case for the Taoist approach for a love-based environmental education. They believe environmental education should be experiential and include contemplative practices: "Contemplative approaches, such as meditation, contemplation, introspection, and reflection, can be effective methods for developing embodied knowledge and fostering love for nature through personal experience," ending their article with this vision: "We need love-based EE to break free from anthropocentric paradigms and truly embrace nature in our heart and mind as our family. Love is an eternal theme, and it is beyond language and race" (1127).

Taoism, Indigenous perspectives, and the teachings on love by Gandhi and King Jr. can help us move forward with a vision that is deeply respectful of nature, the Earth, and the cosmos. They can provide the touchstones of a New Story of education. This vision is not static and will develop and change in the spirit of cosmogenesis as we participate in the unfolding of the universe.

In his last book, *The Great Work*, Berry (1999) describes this unfolding vision:

> We have been told that concern for the environment must become "the central organizing principle of civilization."
>
> The story of the universe is now being told as the epic story of evolution by scientists. We begin to understand our human identity with all the other modes of existence that constitute with us the single universe community. The

one story includes us all. We are, everyone, cousins to one another. Every being is intimately present to and immediately influencing every other being ...

We are now experiencing a moment of significance far beyond what any of us can imagine ... The mythic vision has been set into place. The distorted dream of an industrial technological paradise is being replaced by the more viable dream of a mutually enhancing human presence within an ever-renewing organic-based Earth community. The dream drives the action. In the larger cultural context, the dream becomes the myth that both guides and drives the action. (201)

Berry (1999) acknowledges that there are major challenges to actualizing this New Story but concludes that it is difficult to believe that "the larger purposes of the universe or of the planet Earth will ultimately be thwarted" (200–1).

We need to situate education in the largest possible context, and that is the cosmos. Everything should flow from that. The Tao, Indigenous teachings, and love in all its forms can help in providing this context. They show how we are deeply connected, how we can honour all life and each other, and they provide the framework for the New Story and the Great Work that can address the challenge of climate change and help heal the Earth.

I close this book with this prayer from the Ute people:

Earth teach me quiet ~
as the grasses are still with new light.
Earth teach me suffering ~
as old stones suffer with memory.
Earth teach me humility ~
as blossoms are humble with beginning.
Earth teach me caring ~
as mothers nurture their young.
Earth teach me courage ~
as the tree that stands alone.
Earth teach me limitation ~
as the ant that crawls on the ground.
Earth teach me freedom ~

as the eagle that soars in the sky.
Earth teach me acceptance ~
as the leaves that die each fall.
Earth teach me renewal ~
as the seed that rises in the spring.
Earth teach me to forget myself ~
as melted snow forgets its life.
Earth teach me to remember kindness ~
as dry fields weep with rain.

References

Abeles, Vicki. 2015. *Beyond Measure: Rescuing an Overscheduled, Overtested, Underestimated, Generation*. New York: Simon & Schuster.

Armstrong, Karen. 2019. *The Lost Art of Scripture: Rescuing the Sacred Texts*. New York: Alfred Knopf.

Aurelius, Marcus. 1997. *Meditations*. Translated by George Long. Edited by Willliam Kaufman. Mineola, NY: Dover.

Baring, Anne. 2013. *The Dream of the Cosmos: A Quest for the Soul*. Dorset, UK: Archive.

Berry, Thomas. 1988. *The Dream of the Earth*. San Francisco: Sierra Club Books.

–. 1999. *The Great Work: Our Way into the Future*. New York: Three Rivers Press.

Beilock, Susan. 2015. *How the Body Knows Its Mind: The Surprising Power of the Physical Environment to Influence How You Think and Feel*. New York: Atria.

Boldt, Laurence G. 1999. *The Tao of Abundance: Eight Ancient Principles for Abundant Living*. New York: Penguin/Arkana.

Cajete, Gregory. 1994. *Look to the Mountain: An Ecology of Indigenous Education*: Rio Rancho, NM: Kivaki Press.

Carson, Rachel. 1962. *Silent Spring*. London: Hamish Hamilton.

Chan, Wing-tsit, ed. and trans. 1963. "The Humanism of Confucius." In *A Source Book in Chinese Philosophy*, 14–48. Princeton, NJ: Princeton University Press.

Cherney, Isabelle D., Lisa Kelly-Vance, Katrina Gill Glover, Amy Ruane, and Brigette Oliver Ryalls. 2003. "The Effects of Stereotyped Toys and Gender on Play Assessment in Children Aged 18–47 Months." *Educational Psychology* 23: 95–106. https://doi.org/10.1080/01443410303222.

Chuang Tsu. 1974. *Inner Chapters*. Translated by Gia-fu Feng and Jane English. New York: Vintage Books.

Cleary, Thomas. 2003a. *Sex, Health, and Long Life: Manual of Taoist Practice*. In *The Taoist Classics: The Collected Translations of Thomas Cleary*, edited by Thomas Cleary, vol. 1, 414–86. Boston: Shambhala Publications.

–. 2003b. *Vitality, Energy, Spirit: A Taoist Sourcebook.* In *The Taoist Classics: The Collected Translations of Thomas Cleary,* edited by Thomas Cleary, vol. 3, 1–52. Boston: Shambhala Publications.

–. 2003c. *Wen-tzu: Understanding the Mysteries.* In *The Taoist Classics: The Collected Translations of Thomas Cleary,* edited by Thomas Cleary, vol. 1, 141–302. Boston: Shambhala Publications.

Csikszentmihalyi, Mihaly. 1990. *Flow: The Psychology of Optimal Experience.* New York: HarperCollins Publishers.

Cui, Huaizu, and Qingqing Hu. 2015. "Creation and Appreciation of 'Nature and Man in One' and Chinese Classic Beauty of Garden – Taking the Suzhou Classic Garden as an Example." *SHS Web of Conferences* 17, Art. 02001. https://www.shs-conferences.org/articles/shsconf/pdf/2015/04/shsconf_icmetm2015_02001.pdf.

Culham, Tom. 2013. *Ethics Education of Business Leaders: Emotional Intelligence, Virtues, and Contemplative Learning.* Charlotte, NC: Information Age Publishing.

Culham, Tom, and Jing Lin. 2020. *Daoist Qi and Virtue Cultivation for Immortality: Insights for Deep Learning in Contemporary Education.* Charlotte, NC: Information Age Publishing.

Davidson, Richard J., and Sharon Begley. 2012. *The Emotional Life of Your Brain.* New York: Hudson Street Press.

De Bary, William Theodore, and Irene Bloom. 1999. *Sources of Chinese Tradition: From Earliest Times to 1600.* New York: Columbia University Press.

Delio, Ilia. 2016. *The Unbearable Wholeness of Being: God, Evolution, and the Power of Love.* Maryknoll, NY: Orbis Books.

Deresiewicz, William. 2014. *Excellent Sheep: The Miseducation of the American Elite and the Way to a Meaningful Life.* New York: Free Press.

Dombro, Amy Laura, Judy Jabion, and Charlotte Stetson. 2011. *Powerful Interactions: How to Connect with Children to Extend Their Learning.* Washington, DC: National Association for the Education of Young Children.

Emerson, Ralph Waldo. 1968. *The Selected Writings of Ralph Waldo Emerson.* Edited by Brooks Atkinson. New York: The Modern Library.

Equinox Holistic Alternative School (EHAS). 2017/2018. "Staff Handbook." Toronto: Equinox Holistic Alternative School.

Four Arrows, and Jack Miller. 2012. "To Name the World: A Dialogue about Holistic Education and Indigenous Education." *Encounter* 25 (3): 1–11. https://doi.org/10.3138/9781487519506-016.

Galinsky, Ellen. 2009. Interview by Jessica Wiederhorn. Fred Rogers Oral History Collection. Fred Rogers Center for Early Learning and Children's Media at St. Vincent College. Video.

Gandhi, Mahatma. 1980. *All Men Are Brothers: Autobiographical Reflections.* Edited by K. Kripalani. New York: Continuum.

Gandhi, Rajmohan. 2008. *Gandhi: The Man, His People, and the Empire*. Berkeley: University of California Press.

Griffin, Robert. 1977. "Discipline: What's It Taking Out of You?" *Learning*, 77–80.

Grigg, Ray. 1994. *The Tao of Zen*. Rutland, VT: Tuttle.

Herrigel, Eugen. 1971. *Zen in the Art of Archery*. New York: Vintage.

Hirsch, Edward D., Jr., Joseph F. Kett, and James Trefil. 1988. *The Dictionary of Cultural Literacy: What Every American Needs to Know*. Boston: Houghton Mifflin.

Howe, Randy. 2003. *The Quotable Teacher*. Guilford, CT: Lyons Press.

Hutcherson, Cendri A., Emma M. Seppala, and James J. Gross. 2008. "Loving-kindness Meditation Increases Social Connectedness." *Emotion, Space and Society* 8, no. 5: 720–4. https://doi.org/10.1037/a0013237.

Huxley, Aldous. 1956. *Adonis and the Alphabet*. London: Chatto and Windus.

–. 1960. *The Doors of Perception & Heaven and Hell*. London: Chatto and Windus.

–. 1962. *Island*. London: Chatto and Windus.

Kabat-Zinn, Jon. 2005. *Where You Go There You Are: Mindfulness Meditation in Everyday Life*. New York: Hachette.

Kaufman, Sarah. 2016. *The Art of Grace: On Moving Well Through Life*. New York: W.W. Norton.

Kaufman, Stephen K. 1998. *The Living Tao: Meditations on the Tao Te Ching to Empower Your Life*. Boston: Charles Tuttle.

Kelly, Loch. 2019. *The Way of Effortless Mindfulness: A Revolutionary Guide for Living and Awakened Life*. Boulder, CO: Sounds True.

King, Maxwell. 2018. *The Good Neighbor: The Life and Work of Fred Rogers*. New York: Abrams.

Knoblock, John. 1990. *Xunzi: A Translation and Study of the Complete Works*. Vol. 2, Books 7–16. Stanford, CA: Stanford University Press.

Lerner, Michael. 2000. *Spirit Matters*. Charlottesville, VA: Hampton Roads.

Leung, Rachel. 2019. "Famed Architect I.M. Pei's Legacy Stands Tall in Hong Kong through Bank of China Tower." *South China Morning Post*, 17 May. https://www.scmp.com/news/hong-kong/article/3010698/hong-kong-famed-architect-im-peis-legacy-stands-tall-through-bank.

Lillard, Angeline S. 2013. "Playful Learning and Montessori Education." *American Journal of Play* 5: 157–86.

Lin, Jing. 2006. *Love, Peace and Wisdom in Education: A Vision for Education for the 21st Century*. Lanham, MD: Rowman & Littlefield.

Makransky, John. 2007. *Awakening through Love: Unveiling Your Deepest Goodness*. Boston: Shambhala Publications.

McGilchrist, Iain. 2009. *The Master and His Emissary: The Divided Brain and the Making of the Western World*. New Haven, CT: Yale University Press.

McNamee, Gillian Dowley. 2015. *High-Performing Preschool: Story Acting in Head Start Classrooms*. Chicago: University of Chicago Press.

Merton, Thomas. 1965. *The Way of Chuang-tzu*. New York: New Directions.

Michaels, Sarah, Andrew W. Shouse, and Heidi A. Schweingruber. 2008. *Ready, Set, Science! Putting Research to Work in K-8 Science Classrooms*. Washington, DC: National Academy.

Miller, Edward, and Joan Almon. 2009. *Crisis in the Kindergarten: Why Children Need to Play in School*. College Park, MD: Alliance for Childhood.

Miller, John P. 2000. *Education and the Soul: Toward a Spiritual Curriculum*. Albany, NY: SUNY Press.

–. 2006. *Educating for Wisdom and Compassion: Creating Conditions for Timeless Learning*. Thousand Oaks, CA: Corwin.

–. 2010. *Whole Child Education*. Toronto: University of Toronto Press.

–. 2014. *The Contemplative Practitioner: Meditation in Education and the Workplace*. Toronto: University of Toronto Press.

–. 2016. "Equinox: Portrait of a Holistic School." *International Journal of Children's Spirituality* 21, no. 3–4: 283–301. https://doi.org/10.1080/1364436X.2016.1232243.

–. 2017. "Jack Miller on Holistic Education, Oslo." YouTube, 22 October. https://www.youtube.com/watch?v=3q4HVnAuQ6w&t=85s.

–. 2018. *Love and Compassion: Exploring Their Role in Education*. Toronto: University of Toronto Press.

–. 2019a. *The Holistic Curriculum*. Toronto: University of Toronto Press.

–. 2019b. "The Tao of Teaching and Learning." Keynote Address to the Asia Pacific Holistic Education Network Meeting in Seoul, Korea, October.

Miller, John P., and Aya Nozawa. 2002. "Meditating Teachers: A Qualitative Study." *Journal of In-service Education* 28, no. 1: 179–92. https://doi.org/10.1080/13674580200200177.

Miller, John P., Kelli Nigh, Marni J. Binder, Bruce Novak, and Sam Crowell. 2019. *International Handbook of Holistic Education*. New York: Routledge.

Miller, John P., and Wayne Seller. 1985. *Curriculum: Perspectives and Practice*. New York: Longman.

Minford, John, trans. and ed. 2018. *Tao Te Ching*. New York: Viking.

Mitchell, Edgar. 1996. *The Way of the Explorer*. New York: Putnam.

Mitchell, Stephen, trans. 1988. *Tao Te Ching*. New York: Harper Collins.

Montessori, Mario. 1992. *Education for Human Development: Understanding Montessori*. Oxford: Clio.

Nagel, Greta. 1994. *The Tao of Teaching*. New York: Donald Fine Company.

Nagler, Michael N., and Stephanie N. Van Hook. 2019. *Nonviolence Daily: 365 Days of Inspiration from Gandhi*. Petaluma, CA: Person Power Press.

Nakagawa, Yoshiharu. 2002. "Aldous Huxley: A Quest of Perennial Education."
In *Nurturing Our Wholeness: Perspectives on Spirituality in Education*, edited
by John Miller and Yoshiharu Nakagawa, 140–63. Brandon, VT: Foundation for
Educational Renewal.

Ni, Hua-Ching. 1997. *Entering the Tao: Master Ni's Guidance for Self-Cultivation*.
Boston: Shambhala Publications.

Noddings, Nel. 2003. *Happiness and Education*. New York: Cambridge University
Press.

O'Donohue, John. 1999. *Eternal Echoes: Celtic Reflections on Our Yearning to
Belong*. New York: Harper Perennial.

Olds, Anita Rui. 2001. *Child Care Design Guide*. New York: McGraw-Hill.

Palandri, Angela Jung. 1988. "The Taoist Vision. A Study of Tao Yuan-Ming's
Nature Poetry." *Journal of Chinese Philosophy* 15, no. 2: 97–121, https://doi.org
/10.1111/j.1540-6253.1988.tb00593.x.

Paley, Vivian Gussin. 2003. *You Can't Say You Can't Play*. Cambridge, MA:
Harvard University Press.

Quindlen, Anna. 2005. "Testing: One, Two, Three." *Newsweek*, 12 June. https://www
.newsweek.com/testing-one-two-three-119621.

Ricard, Matthieu. 2020. "Women for Positive Change" (blog), 2 March. https://
www.matthieuricard.org/en/blog/posts/women-for-positive-change.

Rohr, Richard. 2013. *Immortal Diamond: The Search for Our True Self*. San
Francisco: Jossey-Bass.

Roth, Harold D. 1999. *Original Tao: Inward Training (Nei-yeh)*. New York:
Columbia University Press.

Secretan, Lance. H. 1996. *Reclaiming Higher Ground: Creating an Organizations
that Inspire Soul*. Toronto: MacMillan.

Slingerland, Edward. 2014. *Trying Not to Try: The Art and Science of Spontaneity*.
New York: Crown.

Smalley, Susan L., and Diana Winston. 2010. *Fully Present: The Science, Art and
Practice of Mindfulness*. Boston: Da Capo Press.

Spring, Joel .1999. *Wheels in the Head*. 2nd ed. New York: McGraw-Hill College.

Steiner, Rudolf. 1976. *Practical Advice for Teachers: Fourteen Lectures Given at the
Foundation of the Waldorf School Stuttgart, from 21 August to 5 September 1919*.
London: Rudolf Steiner Press.

Strasser, Janis, and Lisa Mufson Koeppel. 2010. "Block Building and Make-believe
for Every Child." *Teaching Young Children* 3, no. 3: 14–15. http://www.naeyc.org
/yc/files/yc/file/201503/YC0315_Tepylo.pdf.

Sun, Youzhi, Yi Zhao, Steve An Xue, and Jianping Chen. 2018. "The Theory
Development of Traditional Chinese Medicine Constitution: A Review." *Journal*

of Traditional Chinese Medical Sciences 5, no. 1: 16–28. https://doi.org/10.1016
/j.jtcms.2018.02.007.

Suzuki, Shunryu. 1973. *Zen Mind, Beginner's Mind*. Tokyo: Weatherhill.

Swimme, Brian, and Mary Evelyn Tucker. 2011. *Journey of the Universe*. New
Haven, CT: Yale University Press.

Swimme, Brian, and Thomas Berry. 1992. *The Universe Story*. New York:
HarperCollins Publishers.

Teilhard de Chardin, Pierre. 1968. *Science and Christ*. New York: Harper & Row.

Tolle, Eckhart. 2005. *A New Earth: Awakening to Your Life's Purpose*. New York:
Dutton

Tucker, Mary Evelyn, John Grim, and Andrew Angyal. 2019. *Thomas Berry:
A Biography*. New York: Columbia University Press.

Van Hook, Stephanie. 2015. "Reframing Masculinity" – Daily Metta, 7 December.
Metta Center for Nonviolence. https://mettacenter.org/daily-metta
/reframing-masculinity/.

Wagamese, Richard. 2016. *Embers: One Ojibway's Meditations*. Madeira Park, BC:
Douglas &McIntyre.

Wallas, Graham. 1926. *The Art of Thought*. London: Watts.

Wang, Jianyu, and L. Allison Stringer. 2011. "The Impact of Taoism on Chinese
Leisure." *World Leisure Journal* 42, no. 3: 33–41. https://doi.org/10.1080/044
19057.2000.9674194.

Wang, Rongpei. 2000. *A Comparative Study of Tao Yuanming's Poetry*. Beijing:
Foreign Language Teaching and Research Press.

Watson, Burton, trans. 1968. *The Complete Works of Chuang Tzu*. New York:
Columbia University Press.

Watts, Alan. 1995. *The Tao of Philosophy*. Boston: Charles Tuttle.

–. 1999. *Taoism: Way Beyond Seeking*. London: Thorson.

Weiming, Tu, and Mary Evelyn Tucker, eds. 2004. *Confucian Spirituality*. New
York: Herder and Herder.

Winston, Diana. 2019. *The Little Book of Being: Practices and Guidance for
Uncovering Your Natural Awareness*. Boulder, CO: Sounds True.

Wolf, Aline. 2004. "Maria Montessori Cosmic Education as a Non-Sectarian
Framework for Nurturing Children's Spirituality." Paper presented at the
ChildSpirit Conference, Pacific Grove, CA.

Wong, Eva, trans. 1997. *The Shambhala Guide to Taoism: A Complete Introduction
to the History, Philosophy, and Practice of an Ancient Chinese Spiritual Tradition*.
Boston: Shambhala Publications.

–, ed. and trans. 2015. *Being Taoist: Wisdom for Living a Balanced Life*. Boston:
Shambhala Publications.

Woodward, Elizabeth. 1935. *Personality Preferred! How to Grow Up Gracefully.* New York: Harper & Brothers.

Yang, Fan. 2018. "Taoist Wisdom on Individualized Teaching and Learning – Reinterpretation through the Perspective of Tao Te Ching." *Educational Philosophy and Theory* 51, no. 1: 117–27. https://doi.org/10.1080/00131857.2018.1464438.

Yang, Fan, Jing Lin, and Thomas Culham. 2019. "From Intimidation to Love: Taoist Philosophy and Love-Based Environmental Education." *Educational Philosophy and Theory* 51, no. 11: 1117–29. https://doi.org/10.1080/00131857.2018.1564659.

Ywahoo, Dhayni. 1987. *The Voices of Our Ancestors: Cherokee Teaching from the Wisdom Fire.* Boston: Shambhala Publications.

Index